Weekly Lesson Tests in FCAT Format Copying Masters

Grade 5

Harcourt School Publishers

www.harcourtschool.com

Copyright © by Harcourt, Inc.

All rights reserved. No part of this publication may be reproduced or transmitted in any form or by any means, electronic or mechanical, including photocopy, recording, or any information storage and retrieval system, without permission in writing from the publisher.

Permission is hereby granted to individuals using the corresponding student's textbook or kit as the major vehicle for regular classroom instruction to photocopy entire pages from this publication in classroom quantities for instructional use and not for resale. Requests for information on other matters regarding duplication of this work should be addressed to School Permissions and Copyrights, Harcourt, Inc., 6277 Sea Harbor Drive, Orlando, Florida 32887-6777. Fax: 407-345-2418.

HARCOURT and the Harcourt Logo are trademarks of Harcourt, Inc., registered in the United States of America and/or other jurisdictions.

Printed in the United States of America

ISBN 10 0-15-380200-6   ISBN 13 978-0-15-380200-3

5 6 7 8 9 10   862   16 15 14 13 12 11 10 09

If you have received these materials as examination copies free of charge, Harcourt School Publishers retains title to the materials and they may not be resold. Resale of examination copies is strictly prohibited and is illegal.

Possession of this publication in print format does not entitle users to convert this publication, or any portion of it, into electronic format.

Contents

© Harcourt • Grade 5

Contents

© Harcourt • Grade 5

Contents

© Harcourt • Grade 5

Name _____

Selection Comprehension

▶ Choose the best answer for each question.

1. What is the MAIN problem in "Rope Burn"?
   - Ⓐ Richard is unhappy because he has to move.
   - Ⓑ Richard is afraid of calling attention to himself.
   - Ⓒ Richard has trouble making friends at his new school.
   - Ⓓ Richard is worried about climbing a rope in gym class.

2. How do you know that "Rope Burn" is realistic fiction?
   - Ⓕ The characters are real people from history.
   - Ⓖ It has a setting that is familiar to most readers.
   - Ⓗ The story events could not happen in real life.
   - Ⓘ It gives instructions for completing a task.

3. Which word BEST describes Richard at the beginning of "Rope Burn"?
   - Ⓐ cautious
   - Ⓑ excited
   - Ⓒ loyal
   - Ⓓ proud

4. Which action BEST shows that Richard is worried about his physical education test?
   - Ⓕ He counts off by fours.
   - Ⓖ He breaks out into a cold sweat.
   - Ⓗ He spends time on the balance beam.
   - Ⓘ He goes to get his lunch from his locker.

5. Why is Richard angry when he first visits James's yard?
   - Ⓐ James has also invited Roland.
   - Ⓑ Richard is jealous of James's big tree house.
   - Ⓒ Richard thinks James wants to embarrass him.
   - Ⓓ James has not finished the book he borrowed.

© Harcourt • Grade 5

6. What can you tell about James?

   (F) He is good at running laps.

   (G) He has moved to a new school before.

   (H) He can understand someone else's feelings.

   (I) He likes Roland more than he likes Richard.

7. Which sentence BEST tells why Richard is grateful to James at the end of the story?

   (A) James gave Richard a rookie card.

   (B) James encouraged Richard to keep trying.

   (C) James let Richard practice at his tree house.

   (D) James told Richard his mistakes in climbing.

8. What lesson does Richard learn in the story?

   (F) Climbing a rope can be hard.

   (G) Tree houses can be fun places to play.

   (H) Moving to a new school can be difficult.

   (I) Friends can help you if you let them.

Written Response

9. **COMPARING TEXTS** Explain why you would or would not like to have a tree house. Use details from BOTH "Rope Burn" and "Tree Houses for Everyone" to support your answer.

   _____

   _____

   _____

   _____

Name _____

Focus Skill: Plot: Conflict and Resolution

▶ **Read the passage. Then choose the best answer for each question.**

Carmen's Rainy Day

There was almost nothing Carmen loved more than rainy Saturdays. Her family members would always gather around and play a board game together on days like today. This morning, when she looked outside and observed the drizzly weather, Carmen ran to the cupboard and selected a game. She cleared off the kitchen table and arranged the game board. Then, she went to collect her father and her two sisters.

Unfortunately, all of Carmen's family members were consumed with chores. Carmen had already cleaned her room, but Isabel and Juana were hard at work cleaning theirs. Carmen's father was compiling a grocery list. Carmen was disappointed that no one could play with her.

Then Carmen came up with a brilliant idea. She darted up to her sisters' room and began helping them. She hung all of their clean clothes in the closet, dusted the furniture, and made Isabel's bed. Then, Carmen ran downstairs to the kitchen to assist her father with his grocery list. She looked in the cabinets and told him what items were needed. With Carmen's help, he quickly completed his list.

Thanks to Carmen, the weekend chores were done. This put everyone in a good mood. Best of all, the family had time to play its favorite game. Isabel and Juana gave Carmen a big embrace. Carmen's father said that he was very proud of her for being so helpful. Carmen knew that this would be the best rainy day of all.

Name _____

1. What is the conflict in the story?

   (A) Carmen and her sisters cannot agree on a game to play.

   (B) Carmen does not want to go grocery shopping with her father.

   (C) Carmen wants to play with her family, but everyone is busy.

   (D) Carmen hates to spend her weekends cleaning the house.

2. Which sentence from the story summarizes the conflict?

   (F) "Isabel and Juana were hard at work cleaning theirs."

   (G) "Carmen was disappointed that no one could play with her."

   (H) "With Carmen's help, he quickly completed his list."

   (I) "Carmen knew that this would be the best rainy day of all."

3. What is the resolution of the conflict in this story?

   (A) Carmen chooses a board game and sets it up on the kitchen table.

   (B) Carmen helps her family members finish their chores so that they can play.

   (C) Carmen promises to help Isabel and Juana after they play the game.

   (D) Carmen searches the cabinets for food that the family needs.

4. Which sentence from the story summarizes the resolution?

   (F) "She darted up to her sisters' room and began helping them."

   (G) "Unfortunately, all of Carmen's family members were consumed with chores."

   (H) "She looked in the cabinets and told him what items were needed."

   (I) "Thanks to Carmen, the weekend chores were done."

Focus Skill: Plot: Conflict and Resolution

TOTAL SCORE: _____ /4

© Harcourt • Grade 5

Name _____

Narrative Forms

▶ **Choose the best answer for each question.**

1. Which type of story includes characters with exaggerated abilities?
   - Ⓐ a tall tale
   - Ⓑ a myth
   - Ⓒ a fable
   - Ⓓ a folktale

2. Which is an example of historical fiction?
   - Ⓕ a story that teaches children to tell the truth
   - Ⓖ a story that describes a teacher's first day with his class
   - Ⓗ a story that explains why ocean water is salty
   - Ⓘ a story about a family that settled in Arizona in the 1800s

3. Which type of story often includes animal characters that can speak?
   - Ⓐ realistic fiction
   - Ⓑ a fable
   - Ⓒ historical fiction
   - Ⓓ a play

4. Which is an example of realistic fiction?
   - Ⓕ a story about how Fox and Rabbit race to catch the Sun
   - Ⓖ a story about a girl who travels back in time to the Civil War
   - Ⓗ a story about a boy whose grandmother teaches him to cook
   - Ⓘ a story about how the stars came to be so high in the sky

Narrative Forms

© Harcourt • Grade 5

Name _____

5. Which type of story tells how something in nature came to be?

Ⓐ a fable

Ⓑ a myth

Ⓒ a folktale

Ⓓ a tall tale

Narrative Forms

10

TOTAL SCORE: _____ /5

Name _____

Robust Vocabulary

▶ **Choose the best word to complete each sentence.**

1. Janelle is a good friend because she is kind and _____.
   - (A) dubious
   - (B) hesitating
   - (C) sincere
   - (D) coaxing

2. Mi-Ling joined the new student who was sitting by herself on the _____ of the cafeteria.
   - (F) sentry
   - (G) fringes
   - (H) expectation
   - (I) illusion

3. When he broke the mirror, Brandon's face showed _____.
   - (A) humiliation
   - (B) expectations
   - (C) determination
   - (D) hesitation

4. The teacher _____ the shy student into giving a short speech in front of the class.
   - (F) humiliated
   - (G) expected
   - (H) hesitated
   - (I) coaxed

Robust Vocabulary

11

Name _____

5. Andrew was happy because the play met all of his _____.

Ⓐ expectations

Ⓑ obstacles

Ⓒ humiliations

Ⓓ fringes

6. Sidney dove from the highest board into the pool without _____.

Ⓕ determining

Ⓖ expecting

Ⓗ hesitating

Ⓘ humiliating

Robust Vocabulary

12

TOTAL SCORE: _____ /6

© Harcourt • Grade 5

Name _____

Grammar: Complete, Declarative, and Interrogative Sentences

▶ **Choose the best answer for each question.**

1. Which is a declarative sentence?
   - (A) Is Ricardo waiting patiently?
   - (B) Ricardo waits patiently.
   - (C) Because Troy won the prize.
   - (D) Because Troy won the prize?

2. Which is an interrogative sentence?
   - (F) Inside Destiny's green bag?
   - (G) Destiny's green bag.
   - (H) Did Louis ask Cho to be his partner?
   - (I) Louis asked Cho to be his partner.

3. Which is a declarative sentence?
   - (A) Beside Clay's desk and under his notebook.
   - (B) Why did Clay put his pen under his notebook?
   - (C) Where did Juanita get the ideas for her story?
   - (D) Juanita is thinking of ideas for her story.

4. Which is a complete sentence?
   - (F) Asked the teacher for extra paper.
   - (G) Stephan asked the teacher for extra paper.
   - (H) When Maya showed me her drawings.
   - (I) Maya's drawings of the high school?

Oral Reading Fluency

Monkeys are occasionally called the acrobats of the animal kingdom because they are thought to be excellent climbers. While this is true for particular monkeys, it is not true for all of them. In fact, there are several different kinds of monkeys.

Monkeys fall into two primary groups. New World monkeys are superb climbers, spending most of their lives in the tops of trees. They can utilize their hands, feet, and tails to grasp tree limbs and bound from tree to tree.

Old World monkeys have smaller faces and noses; some Old World monkeys lack tails. The ones that do possess tails use them for balance, not for climbing. Because they do not climb as expertly, Old World monkeys spend more time on the ground.

All monkeys grow to different sizes, from less than one foot long to over six feet long from head to tail. Their fur might be brown, black, gray, tan, or other colors.

The majority of monkeys live in the tropical forests of Central and South America. In these tropical forests, the weather is consistently warm and the food is plentiful. Some monkeys reside in high mountains, where the climate can be extremely cold. Other monkeys prefer to inhabit dry, hot deserts.

All monkeys share common characteristics, but they are far from identical. While some monkeys may be climbers and others may live on the ground, each kind of monkey has features that make it unique.

Name _____

Selection Comprehension

▶ **Choose the best answer for each question.**

1. How do you know that "Line Drive" is an autobiography?
   Ⓐ It gives facts and information about a topic.
   Ⓑ It has events that could not happen in real life.
   Ⓒ It tells the author's own thoughts and feelings.
   Ⓓ It explains how people and places came to be.

2. Which word BEST describes Tanya?
   Ⓕ timid
   Ⓖ curious
   Ⓗ impatient
   Ⓘ determined

3. What is the problem in "Line Drive"?
   Ⓐ Tanya wants to play baseball with the boys.
   Ⓑ Mark will not let anyone else be pitcher.
   Ⓒ Ricky is too young to play on the team.
   Ⓓ Tanya's mom wants to be a coach.

4. Why does the author compare the pitcher's mound to a throne?
   Ⓕ to show that Mark acts like he's a king
   Ⓖ to describe what the mound looks like
   Ⓗ to explain how baseball is played
   Ⓘ to prove that the mound is high

5. Which detail would be MOST important to include in a summary
   of the story?
   Ⓐ The coach and the fans love Mark.
   Ⓑ Tanya's brothers are named Ricky and Bobby.
   Ⓒ Mark has his name carved in the handle of his bat.
   Ⓓ Tanya's mom teaches her children to play great baseball.

Name _____

6. Why does Mark grin when Tanya does not see his first
   pitch to her?

   (F) He is happy he has someone new to play ball with.

   (G) He does not think Tanya will be able to hit a pitch.

   (H) He is remembering a great pitch he once threw.

   (I) He is glad that Tanya is about to get a hit.

7. Which sentence BEST states the lesson this story teaches?

   (A) Girls keep score better than boys.

   (B) Baseball is a difficult sport to play.

   (C) Girls can play baseball as well as boys.

   (D) Playing catcher is more important than pitching.

8. Which of these would MOST help a reader understand the ideas in
   "Line Drive"?

   (F) learning how to play baseball

   (G) reading a book about sports heroes

   (H) buying a baseball in a sports store

   (I) looking at pictures of baseball bats

 Written Response

9. Explain why "Line Drive" is a good title for this story. Use details from the story
   to support your answer.

   _____

   _____

   _____

   _____

   _____

Focus Skill: Plot: Conflict and Resolution

▶ Read the passage. Then choose the best answer for each question.

The History Test

One afternoon, Mr. Sparks asked Rashan to hand back that week's history tests to the class. Rashan was surprised to see that his paper was the first one in the pile. A proud smile lit up his face when he saw that he had received the top score. His older sister, Alisa, had helped him study, and he couldn't wait to show her the results of their hard work. Rashan placed his paper on his desk and moved on to pass out the rest of the papers.

The next paper in the pile belonged to Rashan's best friend, Calvin. The smile fell from Rashan's face when he noticed that Calvin's paper was covered in red ink. Calvin had received a much lower score than Rashan because, instead of studying, Calvin had gone to the movies. Rashan was too nervous to talk to Calvin for the rest of the day because he was afraid that Calvin might be jealous of his test score.

When Calvin and Rashan were finding their seats on the bus after school, Rashan's backpack slipped off his shoulder and fell to the floor. Calvin picked it up, and he noticed Rashan's test sticking out of a pocket. Calvin pulled it out before Rashan could stop him.

"Wow! You did really well on the test, Rashan!" Calvin said excitedly. "I knew I should have studied as hard as you did. Could we study together next time?"

Rashan was relieved. He was sorry for doubting his friend and thinking Calvin would be jealous of his good score. On the ride home, the two boys began making a study plan for next week's test.

Name _____

1. What conflict did Rashan face?

   Ⓐ He wanted to receive a higher test score than Alisa.

   Ⓑ He thought Calvin would be jealous of his high test score.

   Ⓒ He disliked spending his entire weekend studying for a test.

   Ⓓ He was upset that Calvin had not invited him to the movies.

2. How did Rashan handle his conflict?

   Ⓕ He avoided talking to Calvin for the rest of the day.

   Ⓖ He took his test out of his backpack.

   Ⓗ He told Calvin that everyone had received a low score.

   Ⓘ He walked home instead of taking the bus.

3. How was Rashan's conflict resolved?

   Ⓐ Calvin saw Rashan's paper on the desk.

   Ⓑ Calvin asked how Rashan had done.

   Ⓒ Calvin learned Rashan's test score accidentally.

   Ⓓ Mr. Sparks mentioned Rashan's test score.

4. How did Rashan feel at the end of the story?

   Ⓕ He was unhappy about telling Alisa his test score.

   Ⓖ He wished that Calvin had asked him about his test score.

   Ⓗ He was upset that Calvin had pulled a paper out of his backpack.

   Ⓘ He was relieved because Calvin was not jealous.

Focus Skill: Plot: Conflict and Resolution

TOTAL SCORE: _____ /4

© Harcourt • Grade 5

Name _____

Robust Vocabulary

▶ **Choose the best word to complete each sentence.**

1. Elena did not brag about winning the race because she is not _____.
   Ⓐ conceited
   Ⓑ mortified
   Ⓒ coaxed
   Ⓓ exhilarated

2. When his baseball team won the final game, Jesse was _____.
   Ⓕ coaxed
   Ⓖ exhilarated
   Ⓗ mortified
   Ⓘ designated

3. After forgetting the end of her speech, Nadira felt _____.
   Ⓐ hesitated
   Ⓑ designated
   Ⓒ mortified
   Ⓓ conceited

4. As the best speller in the school, Maurice _____ over the spelling team.
   Ⓕ humiliated
   Ⓖ mortified
   Ⓗ conceited
   Ⓘ reigned

Robust Vocabulary

19

Name _____

5. Emma knew Nick was playing a trick on her when she saw the _____ on his face.

   (A) smirk

   (B) fringe

   (C) maven

   (D) expectation

6. For the field trip, the front of the bus was _____ for fifth graders.

   (F) exhilarated

   (G) reigned

   (H) designated

   (I) hesitated

7. Mr. Harmon is a music _____ because he is a great piano teacher.

   (A) smirk

   (B) maven

   (C) expectation

   (D) fringe

Robust Vocabulary   20   TOTAL SCORE: _____ /7

Grammar: Imperative and Exclamatory Sentences; Interjections

▶ **Choose the best answer for each question.**

1. Which is an imperative sentence?
   - Ⓐ She ran three laps around the field.
   - Ⓑ Run three laps around the field.
   - Ⓒ Running laps is easy for Michelle.
   - Ⓓ Michelle runs faster than anyone!

2. Which is an exclamatory sentence?
   - Ⓕ Jamie helped Megan with her homework.
   - Ⓖ Jamie, please help Megan with her homework.
   - Ⓗ What an unusual flower Wayne found!
   - Ⓘ Wayne found an unusual flower.

3. Which is an imperative sentence?
   - Ⓐ Will Amelia trade papers with Kelly?
   - Ⓑ Amelia wrote such a funny story!
   - Ⓒ Ben placed his pencil on the desk.
   - Ⓓ Place your pencil on your desk when you finish.

4. Which sentence correctly uses an interjection?
   - Ⓕ Wow Alejandro scored a goal.
   - Ⓖ Wow, Alejandro scored a goal!
   - Ⓗ Alejandro scored a goal!
   - Ⓘ Alejandro scored a goal.

Oral Reading Fluency

Maria and her father were preparing to construct a tree house together.
Maria had wished for a tree house for as long as she could recall. She was
incredibly excited about seeing the view from the trees and spending time
with her best friend, Beth. Maria's father whistled merrily as he gathered his
tools. He glanced up at the cloudless sky and assured Maria that it was a
terrific day for building tree houses.

Building the tree house was demanding work. Maria and her father toiled
all morning and took a break only now and then. By lunchtime, Maria and
her father were virtually exhausted, and Maria began to suspect that it was
too big a project for merely two people to complete.

Just as Maria and her father were finishing lunch, they were surprised
by a couple of visitors. Maria's friend Beth and Beth's older brother lumbered
up with a gigantic box of tools. Maria and her father were overjoyed to
see them. Laboring together, their undertaking went much more quickly.
They were able to complete the tree house that afternoon. It was the most
fantastic tree house Maria had ever laid eyes on.

"Isn't it great to have friends?" Maria's father asked. Maria could scarcely
agree more as she scampered up the newly constructed ladder and gazed
out from the tree. The view from the tree house was even better than Maria
had anticipated. She knew she and Beth would spend many afternoons in
the tree house, enjoying the view and playing games together.

© Harcourt • Grade 5

Selection Comprehension

▶ **Choose the best answer for each question.**

1. What is the MAIN reason Chang is unhappy in Mei Mei's family barn?

   Ⓐ He wants to see Yudi and Shen again.

   Ⓑ He wants to go fishing with his father.

   Ⓒ He thinks the buffalo are noisy and smelly.

   Ⓓ He misses the sights and sounds of the river.

2. What is the MAIN problem in "Chang and the Bamboo Flute"?

   Ⓕ Mei Mei shops for things she cannot afford.

   Ⓖ Chang's mother's cooking wok has disappeared.

   Ⓗ Zhao wants to trade pencils for the flute.

   Ⓘ The houseboat has been wrecked.

3. What does Chang plan to do with his flute?

   Ⓐ play it for the people

   Ⓑ sell it to a musician

   Ⓒ trade it for a wok

   Ⓓ give it to Zhao

4. How do you know that "Chang and the Bamboo Flute" is historical fiction?

   Ⓕ The characters do things that could not happen in real life.

   Ⓖ The story gives information about why a person is important.

   Ⓗ The author tells her own personal thoughts and feelings.

   Ⓘ The story is about people, places, and events from the past.

5. What is the MOST LIKELY reason Bo Won tosses a coin in front of Chang?

   Ⓐ He wants to buy Chang's flute from him.

   Ⓑ He wants listeners to give Chang money.

   Ⓒ He wants to hear Chang play a different tune.

   Ⓓ He wants to give Chang money for music lessons.

6. Why does Chang agree to play the flute in the market?

   Ⓕ He wants to play songs the people can sing.

   Ⓖ He wants to prove to Zhao how good it sounds.

   Ⓗ He thinks he can make money by playing music.

   Ⓘ He thinks he might never get to play music again.

7. Which word BEST describes Chang at the end of the story?

   Ⓐ pleased

   Ⓑ playful

   Ⓒ confused

   Ⓓ embarrassed

8. What is the MOST LIKELY reason Chang wants to have his gift wrapped?

   Ⓕ He wants Bo Won to see how pretty it is.

   Ⓖ He thinks his mother might like the paper.

   Ⓗ This is a completely new experience for him.

   Ⓘ The gift will not get scratched if it is wrapped.

Written Response

9. How are Chang and the boy in Bo Won's story ALIKE and DIFFERENT? Use details from "Chang and the Bamboo Flute" to support your answer.

   _____

   _____

   _____

   _____

© Harcourt • Grade 5

Focus Skill: Character's Motives

▶ Read the passage. Then choose the best answer for
each question.

Lourdes's Last Day

For one week every summer, Lourdes went to her Aunt Clarissa's
house on Silver Lake. Every morning when she awoke, Lourdes would
walk out the back door onto Aunt Clarissa's small, sandy beach. She and
her aunt spent every day swimming, catching frogs, and playing in
the sand.

This year, the week seemed to pass very quickly. Before Lourdes knew
it, her last day had arrived. That morning, Aunt Clarissa challenged
Lourdes to a swimming race all the way out to the floating dock and back.
Lourdes sighed and said she would prefer to sit in her chair and watch the
ducks. Her aunt offered to take her fishing, and again Lourdes said she
was not interested.

"You know, Lourdes," said Aunt Clarissa, "I think we should do
something extra special today. How about going for a boat ride to the
other end of the lake? We could take a picnic lunch!" Lourdes couldn't
contain her excitement about her aunt's plan. Soon they had packed their
lunch and had loaded it in the boat.

"I think I am the luckiest person in the world," Lourdes said to her
aunt as they sped through the sparkling water. Lourdes closed her eyes
and felt the warm sun on her face and the cool wind in her hair. She knew
that she would be able to recall the vivid memories of this week whenever
she wanted.

"Aunt Clarissa," she said, "we should do something extra special on
the last day of my summer visit next year, too."

1. Why did Lourdes refuse to swim or fish with her aunt?

   Ⓐ Aunt Clarissa never lets Lourdes choose where to fish.

   Ⓑ Lourdes thinks that swimming and fishing are boring.

   Ⓒ Aunt Clarissa always swims faster than Lourdes.

   Ⓓ Lourdes was disappointed that it was her last day.

2. Why did Aunt Clarissa suggest that they do something extra special?

   Ⓕ She was tired of repeating what they had done all week.

   Ⓖ She could see that Lourdes was upset about leaving.

   Ⓗ She hadn't gone on a picnic in a long time.

   Ⓘ She was ready for Lourdes to return home.

3. Why did Lourdes close her eyes when she was on the boat?

   Ⓐ She was not supposed to see where they were going.

   Ⓑ She was upset about returning home the next day.

   Ⓒ She was enjoying the feeling of the sun and the wind.

   Ⓓ She was very tired because she did not get enough sleep.

4. Why did Lourdes feel lucky at the end of the story?

   Ⓕ She was going to visit her aunt for two weeks next year.

   Ⓖ She was able to spend special time with her aunt at the lake.

   Ⓗ She was the first person in her family to take a boat trip.

   Ⓘ She had won all of the games that she played with her aunt.

Focus Skill: Character's Motives

TOTAL SCORE: _____ /4

© Harcourt • Grade 5

Name _____

Vocabulary Strategies: Using Words in Context

▶ **Choose the best answer for each question.**

1. Read the sentence.

   **Deshaun had attended numerous basketball games, but Hillary
   had only attended a few.**

   Which is the best definition of *numerous* as it is used in the sentence?

   Ⓐ scheduled

   Ⓑ regular

   Ⓒ many

   Ⓓ earlier

2. Read the sentence.

   **The teacher asked Jin to elaborate on his story by explaining
   what the characters saw and heard.**

   Which is the best definition of *elaborate* as it is used in the sentence?

   Ⓕ begin again

   Ⓖ read aloud

   Ⓗ end differently

   Ⓘ add detail

3. Read the sentence.

   **Many farmers use special fertilizers and large machinery
   to cultivate their crops.**

   Which is the best definition of *cultivate* as it is used in the sentence?

   Ⓐ grow

   Ⓑ store

   Ⓒ choose

   Ⓓ study

Name _____

4. Read the sentence.

> **When Chen crossed the finish line first, he gave
> a triumphant shout.**

Which is the best definition of *triumphant* as it is used in
the sentence?

Ⓕ silencing

Ⓖ rejoicing

Ⓗ disappointing

Ⓘ weakening

© Harcourt • Grade 5

Narrative Forms

▶ **Choose the best answer for each question.**

1. What is an author's purpose for writing a play?
   - (A) to list facts about a subject
   - (B) to entertain the reader
   - (C) to explain a word's meaning
   - (D) to teach an important life lesson

2. Which type of text is a narrative text?
   - (F) a book about polar bears and their habitat
   - (G) directions for setting up a computer
   - (H) a newspaper article about a town meeting
   - (I) a story by a student about meeting her best friend

3. Which type of text is an expository text?
   - (A) a fantasy story
   - (B) an encyclopedia article
   - (C) a diary entry
   - (D) a short story

4. How can you tell that a story is an example of realistic fiction?
   - (F) It mainly uses characters' words to tell a story.
   - (G) It explains how something in nature came to be.
   - (H) It describes events that could really happen.
   - (I) It tells a story that is set in a historical time period.

© Harcourt • Grade 5

5. *Chang and the Bamboo Flute* is an example of which kind of narrative text?

(A) a fable

(B) science fiction

(C) a myth

(D) historical fiction

Narrative Forms

30

TOTAL SCORE: _____ /5

Name _____

Robust Vocabulary

▶ **Choose the best word to complete each sentence.**

1. Tyrell _____ wants to be chosen for the basketball team this year.
   (A) indignantly
   (B) desperately
   (C) grudgingly
   (D) incredibly

2. Jen smiled at the new student even though some of her classmates _____ at him.
   (F) pried
   (G) reigned
   (H) sneered
   (I) mortified

3. As Kate ran to the student who had fallen, she _____ asked Armen to alert a teacher.
   (A) grudgingly
   (B) urgently
   (C) incredibly
   (D) indignantly

4. Aila was disappointed, but she _____ agreed to watch the movie Ethan chose.
   (F) grudgingly
   (G) desperately
   (H) urgently
   (I) indignantly

Robust Vocabulary   31

5. Using all of her strength, Keisha _____ open the old can of paint.
   Ⓐ reigned
   Ⓑ pried
   Ⓒ mortified
   Ⓓ sneered

6. When Thomas called Serena by the wrong name, she looked at him _____.
   Ⓕ desperately
   Ⓖ grudgingly
   Ⓗ indignantly
   Ⓘ urgently

Grammar: Subjects and Predicates

▶ **Choose the best answer for each question.**

1. What is the subject of this sentence?

   Manuel passed the set of markers to Danielle.

   (A) Danielle
   (B) Manuel
   (C) markers
   (D) passed

2. What is the predicate in this sentence?

   Mei's neighbor, Mrs. Kendall, gave her a tomato plant.

   (F) Mei's neighbor
   (G) Mei's neighbor, Mrs. Kendall
   (H) gave her a tomato plant
   (I) a tomato plant

3. What is the predicate in this sentence?

   Crystal and Marcos wrote a story together.

   (A) Crystal and Marcos wrote
   (B) Crystal and Marcos
   (C) a story
   (D) wrote a story together

4. What is the subject of this sentence?

   Dylan's drawings were scattered all over the large table.

   (F) scattered all over
   (G) were scattered
   (H) Dylan's drawings
   (I) the large table

Grammar: Subjects and Predicates   33 | TOTAL SCORE: _____ /4 |

Oral Reading Fluency

Have you ever wondered how cheese is made? Of course, all cheese is made from milk. Cow's milk is the main ingredient in most cheese, but milk from other animals, such as goats or sheep, is also used. More than 400 different kinds of cheese are produced worldwide, each in a slightly different way. However, three basic steps are used to make all types of cheese.

The first step in cheese-making is to pour the milk into a large container and heat it. As the milk is being heated, it must be stirred constantly by people or machines. At this point, an ingredient is added to the milk that helps it form solid chunks called curds. Part of the milk remains as a watery liquid called whey.

The second step in cheese-making is to remove the curds from the whey. For some types of cheese, the curds are heated and stirred again. For other kinds of cheese, the curds are stacked on top of each other, and their weight creates pressure that squeezes out any extra liquid.

The third step is to add salt and place the curds into a mold, which gives the cheese its shape. Then the cheese is left to ripen, or become ready to eat, which takes time and patience. When the time is right, the cheese can be enjoyed with bread, crackers, or fruit!

Selection Comprehension

▶ **Choose the best answer for each question.**

1. How do you know that "The Daring Nellie Bly" is a biography?

   Ⓐ It has a problem that readers must solve.

   Ⓑ The setting of the story is familiar to most readers.

   Ⓒ It gives information about why a person is important.

   Ⓓ Characters' feelings are shown mostly through dialogue.

2. Why did the author write "The Daring Nellie Bly"?

   Ⓕ to explain how difficult it was to be a reporter

   Ⓖ to tell about an exciting trip around the world

   Ⓗ to teach reporters the best way to get story ideas

   Ⓘ to tell the story of a talented and unusual woman

3. Why did Nellie buy a long-lasting dress before beginning her journey?

   Ⓐ She thought the dress would match her long coat.

   Ⓑ She wanted to avoid having to take trunks along.

   Ⓒ She thought the dress would be good for hot weather.

   Ⓓ She wanted to look nice when crowds came to see her.

4. What was Nellie MOST afraid of on her trip around the world?

   Ⓕ fever

   Ⓖ storms

   Ⓗ failure

   Ⓘ shipwreck

5. What was the FIRST problem Nellie had on her trip?

   Ⓐ Her train arrived two hours late.

   Ⓑ She got seasick onboard the ship.

   Ⓒ The *Oriental* was delayed five days.

   Ⓓ Her cabin on the ship filled with water.

6. Which word BEST describes Nellie Bly throughout her life?

(F) ordinary

(G) mysterious

(H) strong-willed

(I) well-behaved

7. According to the mayor of Jersey City, what had Nellie proved?

(A) American women could be strong and independent.

(B) It was possible to go around the world in eighty days.

(C) Ocean travel was safer and faster than travel by train.

(D) Women could travel long distances more easily than men.

8. Which action BEST shows that Nellie was brave?

(F) She ran a huge company.

(G) She wrote a newspaper column.

(H) She invented the first steel barrel.

(I) She went to a war zone as a reporter.

READ
THINK
EXPLAIN

Written Response

9. Explain why Nellie had the respect and affection of those who knew her. Use details from "The Daring Nellie Bly" to support your answer.

_____

_____

_____

_____

Focus Skill: Character's Motives

▶ Read the passage. Then choose the best answer for each
question.

The Poetry Contest

"Listen to this!" Akina read aloud from the local newspaper, "Entries
are now being accepted for the town poetry contest, and writers of all ages
are welcome." Akina added, "Hiroshi, you are the best poet I know, so you
must enter!"

Hiroshi's face fell as he avoided eye contact and said, "Akina, you know
that I don't like having other people read my poems." Akina knew her best
friend wrote beautiful poetry full of spectacular imagery and would win
the contest easily. She tried all afternoon to convince him to enter, but
Hiroshi refused to change his mind. When he left the table to pour a glass
of water, and Akina was certain that he wasn't paying attention to her,
she slipped one of his notebooks containing several of his poems from his
backpack into hers.

One morning, about two weeks later, Hiroshi's mother woke him up
earlier than usual. She was holding the newspaper, and she was excitedly
tapping the arts section with her finger. There, on the front page of the
arts section, one of Hiroshi's poems had been published. His poem had
won first prize! When his mother rushed off to purchase more copies of
the paper, Hiroshi called Akina on the telephone.

"Akina, you are my best friend, and friends are supposed to be honest
with each other!" Hiroshi said as soon as Akina answered the telephone.

"Hiroshi, you're right, and I apologize for not telling you that I entered
one of your poems in the contest. I never meant to upset you, but I knew
that you would never enter the contest on your own," Akina said.

"I realize that you were only trying to help me, Akina," Hiroshi said.
"I guess I should share my poetry with others. But next time, let's both
decide which of my poems I enter, all right?"

Akina agreed wholeheartedly, and the two friends laughed.

© Harcourt • Grade 5

1. Why does Akina take one of Hiroshi's notebooks?
   (A) She wants to read his most recent poems.
   (B) She plans to enter one of his poems in the contest.
   (C) She wants to show the poems to Hiroshi's mother.
   (D) She plans to send his poems to the local newspaper.

2. What do Akina's actions tell you about the type of person she is?
   (F) She wants to help her friend conquer his shyness.
   (G) She pretends to be Hiroshi's friend to steal his poems.
   (H) She is jealous of Hiroshi's talent as a poet.
   (I) She is too shy to enter her own poems in the contest.

3. Why does Hiroshi tell Akina that friends should be honest?
   (A) He is upset that his relatives will read his poem.
   (B) He is sorry that he did not tell her about the contest.
   (C) He guesses that she has entered his poem in the contest.
   (D) He thinks that she will read his poems aloud.

4. Why do Hiroshi and Akina laugh at the end of the story?
   (F) Hiroshi admits that he entered the contest anyway.
   (G) Hiroshi reads Akina some of his funny poems.
   (H) Both want to share their poems with others.
   (I) Both are happy about solving their problem.

Focus Skill: Character's Motives   38   TOTAL SCORE: _____ /4

Name _____

Vocabulary Strategies: Using Words in Context

▶ **Choose the best answer for each question.**

1. Read this sentence.

   **New stores were built near the mall at the south edge of
   town in the commercial zone.**

   Which words in the sentence give a clue to the meaning of
   commercial?
   (A) new stores
   (B) were built
   (C) south edge
   (D) edge of town

2. Read this sentence.

   **The antiques shop has some rare and beautiful nineteenth-
   century cups and saucers.**

   Which words in the sentence give a clue to the meaning of *antiques?*
   (F) shop has
   (G) rare and beautiful
   (H) nineteenth-century
   (I) cups and saucers

3. Read this sentence.

   **On the field trip, the class visited a monument that honored
   soldiers from the Civil War.**

   Which is the best definition of *monument* as it is used in the
   sentence?
   (A) a group of students who are studying history
   (B) a collection of stories about a historical event
   (C) a work of art in memory of a person or an event
   (D) a legal document about the Civil War

Name _____

4. Read this sentence.

> She put her best effort into her final exam, taking time
> to ponder each of her answers.

Which is the best definition of *ponder* as it is used in the sentence?

F share with others

G rush through quickly

H think carefully about

I give wrong information

5. Read this sentence.

> Mr. Miller painted the interior of the house in February;
> when the weather is warm, he will paint the outside.

Which is the best definition of *interior* as it is used in the sentence?

A walls

B inside

C top

D floor

Vocabulary Strategies:
Using Words in Context

TOTAL SCORE: _____ /5

© Harcourt • Grade 5

Name _____

Robust Vocabulary

▶ **Choose the best word to complete each sentence.**

1. Connor believed that all creatures deserve protection so he _____ for animal rights.
   - Ⓐ relented
   - Ⓑ crusaded
   - Ⓒ pried
   - Ⓓ sneered

2. The fallen trees made the hiking trail _____.
   - Ⓕ impassable
   - Ⓖ eccentric
   - Ⓗ disheartened
   - Ⓘ infuriated

3. Salma enjoyed the novel because its main character was exciting and _____, rather than dull and average.
   - Ⓐ impassable
   - Ⓑ eccentric
   - Ⓒ conceited
   - Ⓓ disheartened

4. Justin's team pushed themselves harder to win the game instead of being _____ by losing.
   - Ⓕ designated
   - Ⓖ impassable
   - Ⓗ eccentric
   - Ⓘ disheartened

5. When Shantelle discovered her brother had left her bicycle outside in the rain, she was _____.
   - Ⓐ eccentric
   - Ⓑ infuriated
   - Ⓒ impassable
   - Ⓓ urgent

Robust Vocabulary

41

6. Deepak enjoyed giving presentations, so it did not _____ him when the teacher assigned him a speech.

(F) crusade

(G) sneer

(H) faze

(I) coax

7. Amanda begged her brother until he _____ and told her about the class trip to Canada.

(A) relented

(B) crusaded

(C) infuriated

(D) sneered

© Harcourt • Grade 5

Name _____

Grammar: Complete and Simple
Subjects and Predicates

▶ **Choose the best answer for each question.**

1. What is the simple subject of this sentence?

   The new teacher introduced herself to the class.

   Ⓐ The new teacher
   Ⓑ teacher
   Ⓒ herself
   Ⓓ class

2. What is the complete predicate in this sentence?

   Marc and Aden coaxed the cat to climb down.

   Ⓕ Marc and Aden coaxed the cat
   Ⓖ coaxed the cat
   Ⓗ to climb down
   Ⓘ coaxed the cat to climb down

3. What is the simple predicate in this sentence?

   Everyone in the class finished the test on time.

   Ⓐ on time
   Ⓑ in the class
   Ⓒ finished
   Ⓓ finished the test on time

4. What is the complete subject of this sentence?

   April and Genji walked over to shake hands with Jen and Pat.

   Ⓕ April and Genji
   Ⓖ Genji
   Ⓗ April
   Ⓘ Jen and Pat

**Grammar: Complete and Simple
Subjects and Predicates**

© Harcourt • Grade 5

TOTAL SCORE: _____ /4

Name _____

Oral Reading Fluency

More than one hundred years ago, an enterprising woman named Mary Kingsley traveled from England to visit parts of Africa. Mary was one of the first English women to explore that continent. In fact, she was the first European to trek through some parts of Africa. At that time, only a few European people had voyaged beyond the northern part of Africa. They understood very little about the other areas.

Mary and her brother Charley were raised in England in the 1800s. Mary did not go to school with other children and lived a somewhat secluded life. As she grew older, she had to take care of her ill mother. Mary's father was a doctor who had a great love of travel and adventure. He had Mary study German so she could help him with some of his scholarly work.

When Mary was 30 years old, she finally had an opportunity to see the world. She sailed to West Africa and was the first European to explore parts of Gabon. She collected many things to bring back to England with her. She found many specimens of animals that she had never seen before, and she knew that scientists would want to study the things she discovered. When Mary returned home to England, she wrote about her adventures. Today children can read about Mary, and they too can dream about traveling the world.

Name _____

Selection Comprehension

▶ **Choose the best answer for each question.**

1. Which sentence BEST tells what "It Takes Talent!" is about?
   - Ⓐ Deon, Andres, and Tara are in the school talent show.
   - Ⓑ Deon hosts the school talent show and discovers his own talent.
   - Ⓒ The students have high hopes that their talent show will be a success.
   - Ⓓ Mr. Herbert believes the students in his school have amazing abilities.

2. Most of the conflict in "It Takes Talent!" involves Deon struggling with
   - Ⓕ himself.
   - Ⓖ his friends.
   - Ⓗ the audience.
   - Ⓘ accidental events.

3. What is the MAIN purpose of the narrator's role?
   - Ⓐ to describe what is happening
   - Ⓑ to provide information about the past
   - Ⓒ to comment on what Deon is doing
   - Ⓓ to give hints about future events

4. Why is Michelle nervous?
   - Ⓕ She sees that Andres's Galaxy Goo is melting.
   - Ⓖ She is afraid she will forget part of her solo.
   - Ⓗ She thinks Grumpy will interfere with her act.
   - Ⓘ She is afraid she will slip on the melted gelatin.

5. Which of these BEST describes Deon?
   - Ⓐ gifted builder
   - Ⓑ talented artist
   - Ⓒ quick thinker
   - Ⓓ good actor

6. What is the purpose of the chorus in "It Takes Talent!"?

(F) to express the characters' thoughts

(G) to introduce the different characters

(H) to explain what the actors are doing

(I) to help students remember their lines

7. Why does Deon refuse to be in the show at first?

(A) He thinks being an emcee is a small role.

(B) He does not want to embarrass himself.

(C) He knows that the show will be bad.

(D) He does not want to show off.

8. Why does Deon say ". . . Grumpy likes to . . . hog the spotlight"?

(F) to make an awkward situation seem funny

(G) to explain that Grumpy is really a pig

(H) to prove that Grumpy is a good actor

(I) to make Rob feel proud of his pig

Written Response

9. Which character in "It Takes Talent!" do you think seems the most like a real person? Identify the character, and explain why he or she seems real. Use details to support your answer.

_____

_____

_____

_____

Name _____

Robust Vocabulary

▶ **Choose the best word to complete each sentence.**

1. When the singer arrived for the concert, the guards had to _____ the crowd.
   - (A) protest
   - (B) eccentric
   - (C) faze
   - (D) restrain

2. The light show and fireworks made the band concert _____.
   - (F) disheartened
   - (G) genial
   - (H) impassable
   - (I) spectacular

3. During winter, many people are _____ by illnesses such as the flu.
   - (A) restrained
   - (B) stricken
   - (C) fazed
   - (D) exhilarated

4. Marco tried to _____ his fear of speaking to groups by acting in a play.
   - (F) overcome
   - (G) crusade
   - (H) protest
   - (I) sneer

5. Alicia worked _____ to finish her project a day early.
   - (A) dramatically
   - (B) grudgingly
   - (C) feverishly
   - (D) indignantly

© Harcourt • Grade 5

6. Whether he is on stage or on the street, that actor always speaks _____.

   (F) feverishly

   (G) indignantly

   (H) dramatically

   (I) grudgingly

7. The new soccer coach was so _____ that she always had a smile on her face.

   (A) genial

   (B) spectacular

   (C) overcome

   (D) eccentric

8. The teacher expected the students to _____ loudly when he announced the surprise test.

   (F) overcome

   (G) crusade

   (H) protest

   (I) restrain

9. The new movie was a _____, because few people went to see it.

   (A) prognostication

   (B) flop

   (C) smirk

   (D) maven

10. My friends decide what to do on weekends after they hear the weather reporter's _____.

   (F) smirk

   (G) humiliation

   (H) prognostication

   (I) flop

Robust Vocabulary

TOTAL SCORE: _____ /10

Name _____

Selection Comprehension

▶ Choose the best answer for each question.

1. What is the problem in "The Night of San Juan"?
   - Ⓐ The girls must visit José Manuel and his grandma.
   - Ⓑ The girls need to find a way to buy coconut sherbet.
   - Ⓒ Grandma must stay in the apartment and has no friends.
   - Ⓓ José Manuel's grandma won't let him join his friends to play.

2. What is the MAIN reason the girls are afraid of José Manuel's grandma?
   - Ⓕ She has a deep, harsh voice.
   - Ⓖ She seems stern and unfriendly.
   - Ⓗ She never invites anyone to visit.
   - Ⓘ She listens to the radio all the time.

3. Why does José Manuel's grandma keep him inside?
   - Ⓐ He has chores he needs to finish.
   - Ⓑ She thinks it is dangerous on the streets.
   - Ⓒ He needs to raise and lower the food basket.
   - Ⓓ She is afraid he will learn bad habits from others.

4. Which words BEST describe Amalia?
   - Ⓕ foolish and clumsy
   - Ⓖ cautious and dainty
   - Ⓗ clever and brave
   - Ⓘ honest and loyal

5. Grandma telephones Mami because Grandma wants to
   - Ⓐ tell Mami about the girls' dinner.
   - Ⓑ give Mami the recipe for corn fritters.
   - Ⓒ warn Mami that the girls have misbehaved.
   - Ⓓ make sure that Mami knows about the invitation.

**Selection Comprehension
"The Night of San Juan"**
© Harcourt • Grade 5

6. How do you know that "The Night of San Juan" is realistic fiction?

(F) The story setting could be a real place.

(G) The story is about the abilities of a hero.

(H) The story is a mystery that must be solved.

(I) The story has acts that are divided into scenes.

7. What will MOST LIKELY happen the day after the Night of San Juan?

(A) José Manuel will get to go play in the streets.

(B) The family will go to the beach at midnight again.

(C) Mami will invite José Manuel's grandma for corn fritters.

(D) The girls will take another red ball to José Manuel's apartment.

8. Which sentence BEST tells a main theme of "The Night of San Juan"?

(F) News often travels quickly in a small town.

(G) A wish may come true if it is made on a beach.

(H) Good friends can think of ways to help each other.

(I) With practice, a person can learn to do almost anything.

 Written Response

9. Which sister from the story would you MOST like to have as a friend? Use details from "The Night of San Juan" to explain your answer.

_____

_____

_____

_____

_____

Focus Skill: Theme

▶ Read the passage. Then choose the best answer for each
question.

Charla and Naanii

"Charla, I have some information that will affect you," said her
mother. "My writing classes have been rescheduled for evenings, so
you will have to take the bus to Naanii's house after school on those
days." Charla's face fell at the thought of spending so much time at her
grandmother's house while her mother worked and then went to class.
Her mother could sense her disappointment.

"I know you think you will be bored there, Charla," she said.
"However, you'll soon find out that Naanii is a fascinating woman and
you can learn many interesting things from her." But Charla, who thrived
on excitement, thought she would probably be very bored.

When Charla arrived at Naanii's house the following Monday, Naanii
was pleased to see her. Then, as Naanii was disappearing up the stairs,
she told Charla to come upstairs after she had completed her homework.
Charla had a difficult time concentrating on her work because she was
curious about the sounds of squeaky drawers opening and closing and
boxes being moved across floors. When she finished her last assignment,
she bounded upstairs and found Naanii at her desk with an enormous
assortment of pictures spread out before her.

"Excellent, you're finished. Now you can help me with this," Naanii
said. "I'm creating a scrapbook that will portray my life's experiences.

"See these photographs? They were taken during a hiking trip through
the mountains of India. Did you know that is when I met my husband,
your Naana? We got caught in a downpour. What a time that was!"

Charla did not know that Naanii had hiked up mountains in India.

"Tell me about the trip and about Naana," Charla said, as she
wondered what other surprising stories Naanii would share with her.
Charla was eager to hear all of them.

© Harcourt • Grade 5

1. How does Charla feel about spending time at Naanii's house?

    (A) She is excited because Naanii is always doing funny things.

    (B) She is disappointed because she thinks she will be bored.

    (C) She is angry because she does not like to ride the bus.

    (D) She is sad because her mother has a lot of work to do.

2. How can you tell that the story's theme will be about learning from older family members?

    (F) Charla is excited to visit Naanii while her mother is working.

    (G) Charla is disappointed that she has to complete her homework at Naanii's house.

    (H) Charla's mother tells Charla that she has a lot to learn from Naanii.

    (I) Charla's mother lists important lessons that Naanii has taught her.

3. How can you tell that Charla is interested in what Naanii is doing upstairs?

    (A) Charla asks Naanii to tell her what she is working on.

    (B) Charla has a hard time concentrating on her homework.

    (C) Charla calls her mother to find out what Naanii is working on.

    (D) Charla finishes her homework faster than usual.

4. What does Charla learn from staying at Naanii's house?

    (F) Concentrating on homework is important.

    (G) Hiking trips in the mountains are fun.

    (H) It is very difficult to get bored.

    (I) Grandparents have exciting stories to share.

Focus Skill: Theme

52

TOTAL SCORE: _____ /4

© Harcourt • Grade 5

Name _____

Literary Criticism

▶ **Read each passage. Then choose the best answer for each question.**

Better Than Sleep

During the bus ride home on the last day of school, I imagined how fabulous it would be to sleep late the next morning. I was known as the lazy fellow who loved to sleep.

Through the windows of the bus, I gazed upon the majestic Rocky Mountains that rose in the distance. With great anticipation, I was looking forward to my family's vacation in a few days, when we would go hiking and camping in those mountains. However, since my primary interest was sleep, I wondered what sleeping in a tent on the ground would be like. I figured that it would probably not be as comfortable and cozy as my own bed.

This was the time of year when colorful flowers were blooming, so our family ate dinner outside in our backyard garden to enjoy the spectacular view. All through dinner, I yawned and imagined my bed with its smooth, cool sheets. My parents looked at each other and laughed. I wondered why they found my actions so amusing, but I just shrugged my shoulders and went off to bed.

The next morning, I was dreaming that I was having quite a bumpy ride on a bus and that I was being thrown back and forth. Suddenly, I awoke and realized that I really *was* being jostled—my father was shaking me gently but persistently, with a cheerful expression on his face.

"Surprise!" he exclaimed. "We're leaving early for the mountains! Last night, your mother and I decided to leave early this morning in order to spend a little more time seeing the sights!" Wide awake now in the backseat of the car, I wondered whether anything was better than sleep. Seeing the wonders of the Rocky Mountains, perhaps?

1. Which statement describes the passage?
   Ⓐ A father is telling a story about his son.
   Ⓑ A boy is telling a story about himself.
   Ⓒ The writer is telling a story about the past.
   Ⓓ The writer is telling a story about another planet.

© Harcourt • Grade 5

2. What is the author's purpose for writing this passage?

(F) to persuade the reader to get more sleep

(G) to describe how much sleep a person should get

(H) to inform the reader how important getting enough sleep is

(I) to entertain the reader with a story about a boy who loved to sleep

Sojourner Truth

Sojourner Truth was a famous woman who lived during the 1800s. She spoke out against slavery and she spoke for women's rights. Her real name was Isabella Baumfree, but she gave herself the name Sojourner Truth. Her goal was to speak truthfully as she traveled from place to place. The word *sojourn* means to live in a place for only a brief time.

Isabella was born into slavery about 1797. She was freed about 30 years later. She became a preacher and traveled to different places. In Massachusetts, she met other people who were against slavery. She joined their cause. She continued to travel and talk about the evil of slavery. Later, she gave speeches about equal rights for women. She also worked to help people who had once been enslaved.

3. What is the author's purpose in writing this passage?

(A) to entertain

(B) to persuade

(C) to inform

(D) to describe

4. Which statement best explains the author's purpose?

(F) The author gives details about Sojourner Truth's life.

(G) The author tells a funny story about Sojourner Truth.

(H) The author gives details of Sojourner Truth's life in slavery.

(I) The author wants readers to agree with Sojourner Truth.

Literary Criticism

54

TOTAL SCORE: _____ /4

© Harcourt • Grade 5

Name _____

Robust Vocabulary

▶ **Choose the best word to complete each sentence.**

1. After Daniela's team lost the match by one point, she had a _____ look on her face.
   - (A) raspy
   - (B) grim
   - (C) relented
   - (D) swarms

2. At the party, the _____ sang and laughed all night.
   - (F) swarms
   - (G) mavens
   - (H) revelers
   - (I) fringes

3. When he saw the puppy he wanted in the pet shop window, Rodrigo looked _____.
   - (A) raspy
   - (B) grim
   - (C) irresistible
   - (D) wistful

4. Because she loved being in the sunlight, going outside on a sunny day was _____ to Ellen.
   - (F) wistful
   - (G) irresistible
   - (H) raspy
   - (I) grim

Robust Vocabulary   55

© Harcourt • Grade 5

5. When the doors opened for the big sale, everyone crowded around the entrance and _____ into the store.

   (A) infuriated

   (B) swarmed

   (C) relented

   (D) reveled

6. Chen's teacher allowed him an extra day to finish the project, and Chen was _____.

   (F) mortified

   (G) raspy

   (H) grateful

   (I) grim

7. After Jamie cheered for hours at the baseball game, her voice became _____.

   (A) raspy

   (B) grateful

   (C) wistful

   (D) grim

Name _____

Grammar: Compound Subjects and Predicates

▶ **Choose the best answer for each question.**

1. Which sentence contains a compound subject?
   - (A) James ate his dinner, and then he played the piano.
   - (B) James plays the piano and the flute.
   - (C) James played the piano while Marcella ate dinner.
   - (D) James and Marcella both play the violin.

2. Which sentence contains a compound predicate?
   - (F) Claudia and Lucia rode their bicycles; they parked them in the lot.
   - (G) Claudia and Lucia rode their bicycles and parked them in the lot.
   - (H) Claudia and Lucia rode their bicycles to the lot.
   - (I) Claudia rode her bicycle to the lot, and Lucia rode hers.

3. Read the following sentences.

   On Saturday, Lee visited her cousins. Rochelle visited her cousins. Deon visited his cousins.

   What is the best way to combine these three sentences by using a compound subject?
   - (A) On Saturday, Lee, Rochelle and Deon, visited their cousins.
   - (B) On Saturday, Lee, Rochelle, and Deon visited their cousins.
   - (C) On Saturday, Lee, Rochelle, and Deon, visited their cousins.
   - (D) On Saturday, Lee and Rochelle and Deon, visited their cousins.

4. Read the following sentences.

   Kory finished his math homework. He helped his mother.

   What is the best way to combine these sentences by using a compound predicate?
   - (F) Kory finished his math homework, helped his mother.
   - (G) Kory finished his math homework, and Kory helped his mother.
   - (H) Kory finished his math homework and helped his mother.
   - (I) Kory finished his math homework he helped his mother.

Oral Reading Fluency

One summer evening, Raina's father escorted her to the circus. On the way there, he informed her, "This is like no other circus you have seen before." Raina's mind was filled with expectations of all the different animals that she would see.

The circus was set up on the field behind the high school. A large, brightly colored tent was located in the middle, and carts selling food and drinks were lined up around the fringes of the field. Raina's excitement grew as they approached the main tent.

Inside the tent, an exhibit stage was set up in the center, lit by many brightly colored lights. Soon a woman strode onto the stage and said, "Welcome to the Acrobat Circus. Enjoy the show!" Raina asked her father if an acrobat was a type of animal. He laughed and told her she would soon find out.

The tent filled with loud music, and a group of people with painted faces and bright costumes ran up to the stage. They did flips, somersaults, and cartwheels, and they appeared to fly through the air. They balanced on tightropes and swung on swings far overhead. Raina held her breath as she watched, feeling exhilarated. After the show, she told her father that the acrobat circus was better than she had ever imagined.

© Harcourt • Grade 5

Name _____

Selection Comprehension

▶ **Choose the best answer for each question.**

1. How do you know that "When the Circus Came to Town"
   is historical fiction?
   Ⓐ The story events could have happened in the past.
   Ⓑ The characters are actual figures from history.
   Ⓒ The story events could not happen in real life.
   Ⓓ The story gives facts and details about a topic.

2. Why doesn't Ursula want to join the crowd outside?
   Ⓕ She wants to avoid walking in the snow.
   Ⓖ She is embarrassed by the way she looks.
   Ⓗ She wants to join her friends somewhere else.
   Ⓘ She is afraid the wind will blow off her scarf.

3. Why does Ah Sam say his cousins need music?
   Ⓐ They need song words to explain their tricks.
   Ⓑ They need the rhythm in order to do their act.
   Ⓒ They want to put the audience in a good mood.
   Ⓓ They want everyone to clap while they perform.

4. What does it mean when Ursula says "I felt like parrots had landed
   in my home"?
   Ⓕ The townspeople were all dressed up for the circus.
   Ⓖ A large flock of birds had flown into her yard.
   Ⓗ Ah Sam had feathers on his new clothes.
   Ⓘ The cousins' costumes were very colorful.

5. Which idea BEST shows that Ah Sam planned all along for Ursula to
   play her music?
   Ⓐ The cousins have already learned to spell out "Thank you, Ursula."
   Ⓑ Ah Sam suggests that Ursula sneak out to stand behind the crowd.
   Ⓒ Ah Sam says the cousins have a trick no one has seen before.
   Ⓓ The cousins arrive on a stagecoach without a musician.

© Harcourt • Grade 5

6. Ursula forgets to play her music at times during the show because she is

    (F) excited by some of the acts.

    (G) thinking about pirate signals.

    (H) worried about making a mistake.

    (I) concerned about her father's hurt lip.

7. What finally makes "Pirate Ursula" return?

    (A) Mr. Schultz carries her nearer to the fire.

    (B) Her entire pirate crew attends the circus.

    (C) The audience applauds for her music.

    (D) Susie gives her a secret pirate sign.

8. What is the MOST important lesson Ursula learns in the story?

    (F) A circus can take place outdoors.

    (G) People can learn to do amazing tricks.

    (H) Looks are not as important as how you feel.

    (I) Two people can do jumps together in a costume.

Written Response

9. How do Ursula's feelings change during the story? Use details and examples from "When the Circus Came to Town" to support your answer.

_____

_____

_____

_____

_____

Name _____

Focus Skill: Theme

▶ **Read the passage. Then choose the best answer for each question.**

Deron's Note

"Deron," said Michael, "can you come over this afternoon? My grandfather will take us to the airport to watch the planes, and then we can have dinner at the restaurant near the runway!" Deron agreed immediately, and he told Michael that he would ask his father's permission as soon as he got home. Deron smiled all the way to the school bus, and he was still smiling when he sat down next to his friend Chantrea.

"Did you remember to give your note to the bus driver?" Chantrea asked. "The one that says you can get off at my house today?" In his excitement, Deron had forgotten all about his plans with Chantrea. He reached in his back pocket, and he could feel the small, crumpled note from his father. Then he thought about watching the planes. He held out his empty hand to Chantrea and told her that his father had forgotten to write the note.

That afternoon, Deron sat glumly watching the planes and thinking about how he had lied to his good friend. Michael's grandfather, who was very wise, noticed Deron's mood and asked him what was wrong. Embarrassed, Deron told him what he had done.

"Deron, you should always try to correct your mistakes. Why don't you call Chantrea, explain what you did, and ask her to join us?" Deron followed the advice, and the three friends ended up having a wonderful afternoon together.

1. Why does Deron tell Chantrea that his father forgot to write the note?
   - (A) because his father wrote him a note to go to Michael's house
   - (B) because he wants to go to the airport with Michael that day
   - (C) because he is embarrassed that the note was ruined in his pocket
   - (D) because he knows that Chantrea made plans with someone else

© Harcourt • Grade 5

2. What lesson does Deron learn at the end of the story?

(F) Sometimes it is good to lie to your friends.

(G) Friends can help you in difficult times.

(H) It is always best to tell the truth.

(I) Old friends are better than new friends.

3. Why does Michael's grandfather tell Deron to call Chantrea?

(A) He believes that Deron should correct his mistake by telling Chantrea the truth.

(B) He thinks that Deron does not want to go to Chantrea's house the next day.

(C) He wants Deron to describe the sights and sounds of the airport to Chantrea.

(D) He wishes that Michael would also become friends with Chantrea.

4. What is another lesson that Deron learns in the story?

(F) You should never give up on your dreams about the future.

(G) You should never change plans that you make with a friend.

(H) You cannot correct a mistake once you have made it.

(I) Young people can learn from the wisdom of older people.

Focus Skill: Theme

62

TOTAL SCORE: _____ /4

Literary Criticism

▶ **Read the passage. Then choose the best answer for each question.**

The Town Days Parade

Nakeisha woke up early Saturday morning, feeling exhilarated. She had been waiting for months for this day to come. It was the first day of Town Days, a weekend-long celebration of the things that made her town special.

This year, Nakeisha had an important role to play in Town Days. She and her fifth-grade class were walking in the parade. Her friends Matthew and Beth were going to hold the banner that her class had worked on all week. It read "Mr. Daly's Fabulous Fifth-Graders." Nakeisha got ready quickly, and her father drove her to the town hall.

Nakeisha felt a thrill when she saw the colorful banners and heard the excited ruckus around the town hall. She saw the bright red fire trucks that shone like wet apples against the blue sky. She heard kids chattering, dogs barking, and people laughing, and she smelled the sweet scent of freshly baked apple pie.

Suddenly Nakeisha spotted Mr. Daly in the crowd that swarmed the streets in front of the town hall. He saw her and moved out to the fringes of the group, and she saw that he was holding the banner.

"Nakeisha," Mr. Daly said, "Beth couldn't make it today. I'm going to need you to help Matthew hold the banner. Is that all right with you?" Nakeisha smiled so widely that her cheeks hurt. This year's parade was going to be even better than she had imagined.

1. What is the genre of the passage?
   Ⓐ historical fiction
   Ⓑ science fiction
   Ⓒ realistic fiction
   Ⓓ expository nonfiction

© Harcourt • Grade 5

2. What is the author's main purpose of the passage?

(F) to give the reader information about the Town Days celebration

(G) to teach the reader an important lesson about helping others

(H) to persuade the reader to organize a parade in his or her town

(I) to entertain the reader by telling about Nakeisha's experience at Town Days

3. What words does the author use to describe the scene at the town hall?

(A) feeling exhilarated, waiting for months, things that made her town special

(B) fire trucks that shone like wet apples, kids chattering, sweet scent of freshly baked apple pie

(C) hold the banner, smiled so widely that her cheeks hurt, even better than she had imagined

(D) spotted Mr. Daly, moved out to the fringes of the group, holding the banner

4. Why does the author describe the scene at the town hall?

(F) to help the reader imagine what Nakeisha saw, heard, smelled, and felt

(G) to give the reader information about the purpose of the Town Days parade

(H) to explain to the reader why Beth was unable to come to the parade

(I) to describe to the reader what Nakeisha was thinking before the parade

Literary Criticism

TOTAL SCORE: _____ /4

© Harcourt • Grade 5

Robust Vocabulary

▶ **Choose the best word to complete each sentence.**

1. During silent reading time, Manuel _____ Cassidy to get her attention.
   (A) smirked
   (B) nudged
   (C) swarmed
   (D) assured

2. Before the science fair began, the principal went on stage and _____ the official rules.
   (F) assured
   (G) mortified
   (H) proclaimed
   (I) infuriated

3. Because she had studied only briefly, Nisha could not help but _____ about her history test.
   (A) coax
   (B) ruckus
   (C) sneer
   (D) fret

4. Janelle loved to make her friends laugh by dressing up in her most _____ outfits.
   (F) outlandish
   (G) impassable
   (H) proclaimed
   (I) exhilarated

© Harcourt • Grade 5

5. Luis could not fall asleep because his sister and her friends
   were making a loud _____ in the next room.

   (A) fret

   (B) ruckus

   (C) protest

   (D) fringes

6. Chi _____ his mother that he would finish his homework before
   going to Daniel's house.

   (F) relented

   (G) hesitated

   (H) assured

   (I) proclaimed

© Harcourt • Grade 5

Name _____

Grammar: Simple and Compound Sentences

▶ **Choose the best answer for each question.**

1. Which sentence is a simple sentence?

   Ⓐ Nicole wanted to try out for softball, and she persuaded Corrine to join her.

   Ⓑ Nicole and Corrine stayed after school to try out for the softball team.

   Ⓒ Nicole and Corrine played catch together, and they also ran laps to warm up.

   Ⓓ Nicole and Corrine tried out for the softball team, and then they walked home.

2. Which sentence is a compound sentence?

   Ⓕ Tad enjoyed reading stories about animals, space, and travel.

   Ⓖ Tad read a book about space, and then he gave it to Ben.

   Ⓗ Tad drew pictures of stars and other objects in the sky.

   Ⓘ Tad went to the library to return a book and find a new one.

3. Which sentence is written correctly?

   Ⓐ Domingo finished all his homework, but he still had to study for his test.

   Ⓑ Domingo finished all his homework but he still had to study for his test.

   Ⓒ Domingo finished all, his homework, but he still had to study for his test.

   Ⓓ Domingo finished all his homework, he still had to study for his test.

4. Which sentence is written correctly?

   Ⓕ Gina's cat had kittens she invited her friends over to see them.

   Ⓖ Gina's cat had kittens, she invited her friends over to see them.

   Ⓗ Gina's cat had kittens, and she invited her friends over to see them.

   Ⓘ Gina's cat had kittens and she invited her friends over to see them.

**Grammar: Simple and
Compound Sentences**

© Harcourt • Grade 5

TOTAL SCORE: _____ /4

Name _____

Oral Reading Fluency

One morning, while Aaron was waiting for the school bus, he felt
something brush against his legs. He looked down and saw a small cat with
emerald eyes looking up at him while it began to twist its tail around Aaron's
ankles. After a week, Aaron's mother finally allowed him to bring the cat
home to keep as a pet.

Aaron decided to name the cat Stripes, and the two became inseparable.
Every day when he returned from school, Aaron would see Stripes waiting
for him at the top of his driveway. And every day as Aaron would approach
Stripes, the cat would stand and stretch lazily before she wrapped herself
about Aaron's legs.

When he entered the house, Aaron would feed his cat. After several
weeks, Aaron noticed Stripes's stomach was growing larger, and her food
bowl usually needed to be replenished.

One afternoon, Aaron noticed Stripes was not waiting for him when he
got off the bus. He rushed into the house and saw that her food and water
bowls were still full.

He searched the house, but Stripes was nowhere to be found. Suddenly,
Aaron heard a sound in his closet. He flung open the door and spotted
Stripes lying on a pile of clothes feeding four newborn kittens. Aaron
laughed, because he finally understood why Stripes had grown so large.

_____ /WCPM

© Harcourt • Grade 5

Name _____

Selection Comprehension

▶ **Choose the best answer for each question.**

1. Why did the author write "When Washington Crossed the Delaware"?

   (A) to explain how Washington was chosen to be a general

   (B) to tell about important events in our country's history

   (C) to show that Washington would be a good President

   (D) to describe two historical towns in our country

2. How do you know that "When Washington Crossed the Delaware" is narrative nonfiction?

   (F) The characters, places, and events are real.

   (G) The plot has a beginning, a middle, and an ending.

   (H) The author tells her personal thoughts and feelings.

   (I) The story has headings for sections of related information.

3. What is the MOST LIKELY reason Washington wanted to keep his December 26 attack plans a secret?

   (A) He was afraid the men would not want to march to Princeton.

   (B) He hoped they could win the battle if the enemy was unprepared.

   (C) He was uncertain about the possible outcome of the battle.

   (D) He knew his men wanted to go home immediately.

4. What happened RIGHT AFTER Washington and his men crossed the Delaware?

   (F) They tried to slow down the British troops.

   (G) They captured three German regiments.

   (H) They started a long march to Trenton.

   (I) They began fighting the Hessians.

5. Why was the outcome of the Battle of Trenton so important?

   (A) It meant that the troops could move on to Princeton.

   (B) It meant that the British troops would go home at once.

   (C) It gave the Americans hope that they might win the war.

   (D) It gave the Hessians a good reason to go back to Germany.

**Selection Comprehension
"When Washington Crossed
the Delaware"**

© Harcourt • Grade 5

6. What was the MAIN reason crossing the Delaware was difficult?

    Ⓕ the lack of boats

    Ⓖ the tired troops

    Ⓗ the darkness

    Ⓘ the weather

7. What MOST helped the Americans win the Battle of Trenton?

    Ⓐ the size of their army

    Ⓑ the element of surprise

    Ⓒ the number of cannons

    Ⓓ the location of the fight

8. What was the MAIN reason many of Washington's men agreed to stay with him after the Battle of Trenton?

    Ⓕ They wanted the country to be free.

    Ⓖ They wanted to receive the extra pay.

    Ⓗ They knew the march to Princeton would be easy.

    Ⓘ They knew they were winning the war against Britain.

Written Response

9. How do you know that Washington was a good leader? Use details from "When Washington Crossed the Delaware" to explain your answer.

_____

_____

_____

_____

_____

_____

Focus Skill: Text Structure: Sequence

▶ Read the passage. Then choose the best answer for each question.

How to Make a Comic Strip

If you ever want to create a comic strip, follow these simple steps to produce a masterpiece!

First, decide what will happen in your story. Many comic strip stories revolve around a hero with superhuman powers. Use your imagination to write about whatever you find most interesting. Be creative! Next, make a list of all the characters in your story and the main events of the plot. Decide which events will receive a picture. Count the number of pictures you need, and then figure out what will be drawn in each panel of the comic strip to tell the story.

Next, draw each panel picture on a separate sheet of paper. Different techniques can be used to draw your pictures. A popular way to draw is to sketch your scene with pencil, and then draw over the pencil lines with black ink. Once the pictures have been completed, add the words that the characters said or thought in each panel. You can finish each picture by using markers or crayons to add color.

When you have completed your comic strip, put the pages in plastic bags to protect them. Don't forget to show your finished comic strip to friends and family to see how they like your work.

1. What should you do before you begin drawing the comic strip?
   (A) Add the words that the characters say or think.
   (B) Sketch the first drawing of each picture with a pencil.
   (C) Make a list of the characters and events.
   (D) Put the pages in plastic bags to protect them.

2. What should you do after you count the number of pictures needed?

(F) Decide which events will get a picture.

(G) Make a list of the characters and main events.

(H) Decide what picture will be drawn in each panel.

(I) Add the words the characters say.

3. What do you do before you add words to the comic strip panels?

(A) You put the pages in plastic bags.

(B) You use pencil to draw the pictures.

(C) You use black ink over the pencil.

(D) You add color to each picture.

4. What do you do after putting the pages in plastic bags?

(F) Show your finished project to family and friends.

(G) Color the pictures with markers or crayons.

(H) Count the events in the story.

(I) Work on the comic strip after school.

Focus Skill: Text Structure: Sequence

72

TOTAL SCORE: _____ /4

Name _____

Reference Sources

▶ **Choose the best answer for each question.**

1. Which is the best reference source to use to learn about the first mayor of New York City?
   - (A) a dictionary
   - (B) an encyclopedia
   - (C) a thesaurus
   - (D) an almanac

2. Which research question would best be answered by using an atlas?
   - (F) What types of animals live near the South Pole?
   - (G) Who was the first person to discover the South Pole?
   - (H) What are the definitions of the word *pole*?
   - (I) Which countries are closest to the South Pole?

3. Which source could you use to find out when Vermont became a state?
   - (A) a thesaurus
   - (B) a newspaper
   - (C) an almanac
   - (D) a magazine

4. Which question would best be answered by using a thesaurus?
   - (F) Which states border Washington, D.C.?
   - (G) Who was the president of the United States in 1980?
   - (H) What is another word for *thrilling*?
   - (I) What is the root of the word *demonstrate*?

Reference Sources

© Harcourt • Grade 5

5. Which resource would give you the most information about World War II?

(A) a nonfiction book

(B) a dictionary

(C) an atlas

(D) a magazine

6. Where would you look to find yesterday's baseball scores?

(F) an almanac

(G) a thesaurus

(H) a magazine

(I) the Internet

© Harcourt • Grade 5

Name _____

Robust Vocabulary

▶ **Choose the best word to complete each sentence.**

1. Because Joseph had a heavy suitcase, he _____ through the hallway with great difficulty.
   - Ⓐ maneuvered
   - Ⓑ appealed
   - Ⓒ proclaimed
   - Ⓓ coaxed

2. The man stopped and stared because he had never _____ such a large turtle.
   - Ⓕ assured
   - Ⓖ appealed
   - Ⓗ encountered
   - Ⓘ designated

3. Because she remains calm when things go wrong, Melinda is helpful to have around in a _____.
   - Ⓐ destiny
   - Ⓑ maven
   - Ⓒ crusade
   - Ⓓ crisis

4. With such a beautiful voice, Laura's friends believe that it is her _____ to become a singer.
   - Ⓕ destiny
   - Ⓖ ruckus
   - Ⓗ smirk
   - Ⓘ crisis

Robust Vocabulary

75

© Harcourt • Grade 5

5. By cleaning his room without being asked, Antonio is
   _____ his mother that he is responsible.
   - (A) maneuvering
   - (B) persuading
   - (C) proclaiming
   - (D) encountering

6. Even after other runners gave up, Tim showed _____ and finished
   the race.
   - (F) destiny
   - (G) crisis
   - (H) ruckus
   - (I) perseverance

7. The students _____ to their teacher for an extra day to finish their
   projects.
   - (A) maneuvered
   - (B) encountered
   - (C) appealed
   - (D) assured

8. When you go outside in cold weather, several layers of warm clothing
   are _____.
   - (F) crucial
   - (G) crisis
   - (H) grateful
   - (I) eccentric

Robust Vocabulary

TOTAL SCORE: _____ /8

© Harcourt • Grade 5

Grammar: Prepositional Phrases

▶ **Choose the best answer for each question.**

1. Read this sentence.

   The science teacher explained that moths often fly toward light.

   Which of the following is the preposition in this sentence?

   Ⓐ that
   Ⓑ often
   Ⓒ toward
   Ⓓ light

2. Read this sentence.

   Please put your sandwich in your lunch box.

   Which of the following is the object of the preposition in this sentence?

   Ⓕ Please
   Ⓖ your
   Ⓗ sandwich
   Ⓘ lunch box

3. Read this sentence.

   Leah's dog was waiting under the porch.

   Which of the following is the prepositional phrase in this sentence?

   Ⓐ Leah's dog
   Ⓑ was waiting under
   Ⓒ under the
   Ⓓ under the porch

4. Which preposition best completes this sentence?

   Rome is the capital _____ Italy.

   Ⓕ to
   Ⓖ of
   Ⓗ with
   Ⓘ about

Grammar: Prepositional Phrases

TOTAL SCORE: _____ /4

© Harcourt • Grade 5

Oral Reading Fluency

Juanita loved everything about autumn. She loved the colors in the trees and the clean smell of the air. In autumn, Juanita spent as much time as possible enjoying the outdoors.

One afternoon in September, Juanita's father asked her for some assistance in the garden. Juanita agreed and followed him, curious to see what project he had in mind. Her father walked over to the pumpkin patch in the garden where several large pumpkins were growing among the thick tangle of vines. He selected one of the larger pumpkins and twisted it off the stem.

Juanita's father took the pumpkin to his worktable and sliced it in half. The two halves lay on the table, and Juanita looked at its interior, where the pumpkin was soft and wet and full of large white seeds. Juanita helped her father scoop out the seeds from each half of the pumpkin and laid the seeds out on newspapers. Her mouth watered as she realized what was next.

Juanita and her father took the seeds into the kitchen and carefully rinsed them. Then, they placed the seeds in a bowl of salty water where the seeds soaked for several hours. Once the seeds were saturated, they placed the seeds on a pan and roasted them in the oven. By evening, they had tasty pumpkin seeds to share with their family.

© Harcourt • Grade 5

Selection Comprehension

▶ **Choose the best answer for each question.**

1. Why did Charlie want to "give Leonardo his horse"?

   Ⓐ He understood what the horse had meant to Leonardo.

   Ⓑ He wanted to be as great an artist as Leonardo.

   Ⓒ He thought it was Leonardo's best work.

   Ⓓ He wanted to make Leonardo happy.

2. What is the MOST LIKELY reason Nina Akamu was chosen to work on the horse?

   Ⓕ She knew how to work with plaster.

   Ⓖ She had traveled throughout Europe.

   Ⓗ She liked to make models of animals.

   Ⓘ She had studied Renaissance art in Italy.

3. Nina Akamu had to create a new horse because Charlie's horse

   Ⓐ was broken.

   Ⓑ was too small.

   Ⓒ looked strange.

   Ⓓ was made of clay.

4. How do you know that "Leonardo's Horse" is narrative nonfiction?

   Ⓕ The characters, places, and events are real.

   Ⓖ The characters are American folk heroes and legends.

   Ⓗ The story tells where characters are positioned on a stage.

   Ⓘ The story gives details about important events in the author's life.

5. Why did the author write "Leonardo's Horse"?

   Ⓐ to introduce the reader to Leonardo

   Ⓑ to explain to the reader how a statue is made

   Ⓒ to persuade the reader to learn more about Leonardo

   Ⓓ to tell the reader about a special statue that was sent to Italy

6. How did Nina honor Charlie's contribution to the horse?

   Ⓕ She used balloons in Charlie's favorite colors.

   Ⓖ She made a speech when the horse was given to Italy.

   Ⓗ She wrote Charlie's and Leonardo's names on the horse.

   Ⓘ She made the horse's mane especially detailed and beautiful.

7. What did Nina do RIGHT AFTER she made the eight-foot clay horse?

   Ⓐ She worked on the steel skeleton.

   Ⓑ She made an eight-foot plaster horse.

   Ⓒ She sent the clay horse to the foundry.

   Ⓓ She made a twenty-four foot clay model.

8. What can you conclude about Charlie Dent?

   Ⓕ He was generous and creative.

   Ⓖ He had loved horses all his life.

   Ⓗ He was good friends with Leonardo.

   Ⓘ He collected art done by Leonardo.

Written Response

9. **COMPARING TEXTS** How did both Pegasus and Leonardo's horse help fulfill a dream? Use details from BOTH "Leonardo's Horse" and "Bellerophon and Pegasus" to explain your answer.

   _____

   _____

   _____

   _____

   _____

Focus Skill: Text Structure: Sequence

▶ Read the passage. Then choose the best answer for each question.

Stephen's First Football Game

One day in November, Stephen's friend Mulan called to invite him to a football game. Her family rarely missed any of the high school team's games, and Stephen was honored that they had thought of including him. After receiving Mulan's invitation, Stephen marked the date on his calendar in red ink.

The night before the game, Stephen packed a bag with an extra jacket and a pair of sunglasses. Mulan's family picked him up at ten o'clock the next morning, even though the game didn't start until noon. Mulan said there was plenty to see and do beforehand. After they parked the car, they walked around the field. Stephen smelled the various foods being sold by several vendors, and he admired the shirts, hats, and flags for sale. Just before noon, they climbed up into the stands to find their seats.

The competition was fierce, but the game went by so quickly that Stephen was startled when it ended. On the way back to the car, he enthusiastically thanked Mulan and her family for bringing him along. When he looked at Mulan, he noticed that she was hiding something behind her back. Then, she handed Stephen a blue flag with the high school team's name on it.

"It's for you," Mulan explained, "to wave at next week's game. I left the stands and bought it for you right before the game ended. You were so busy cheering that you didn't even notice I had gone!" Stephen was very grateful to have the flag — and to have another date to mark on his calendar in red ink.

1. When did Stephen mark the date of the game on his calendar?
   - (A) after Mulan invited him
   - (B) after he packed his bag
   - (C) the day after the game
   - (D) before Mulan invited him

2. What was the first thing Stephen did after he got to the football field?

(F) smelled the food being sold

(G) thanked Mulan and her family

(H) climbed into the stands to find a seat

(I) walked around the field

3. When did Mulan buy the flag for Stephen?

(A) before the game had started

(B) near the end of the game

(C) at a game the week before

(D) during the middle of the game

4. When will Stephen and Mulan go to another game?

(F) that same evening

(G) the next day

(H) in one week

(I) in two weeks

Focus Skill: Text Structure: Sequence

82

TOTAL SCORE: _____ /4

Name _____

Reference Sources

▶ **Choose the best answer for each question.**

1. Read this question.

   Through how many states does the Mississippi River flow?

   Which would be the best reference source to answer the question above?

   (A) a newspaper

   (B) an almanac

   (C) a dictionary

   (D) an atlas

2. Which would be the best source to use to find a synonym for *implore*?

   (F) a thesaurus

   (G) a newspaper

   (H) a nonfiction book

   (I) a dictionary

3. Read this question.

   What happened this week in London, England?

   Which would be the best reference source to answer the question above?

   (A) a newspaper

   (B) an encyclopedia

   (C) a nonfiction book

   (D) a dictionary

4. Which would be the best source to use to find information about President James Monroe?

   (F) an atlas

   (G) an almanac

   (H) an encyclopedia

   (I) a dictionary

Reference Sources

83

© Harcourt • Grade 5

5. Read this question.

At what time will the sun rise on January 1 next year in Bar Harbor, Maine?

Which would be the best reference source to answer the question above?

(F) a thesaurus

(G) an encyclopedia

(H) an almanac

(I) an atlas

© Harcourt • Grade 5

Name _____

Robust Vocabulary

▶ **Choose the best answer for each question.**

1. Because it has a very long neck and a small body, a giraffe may appear out of _____.
   - (A) gesture
   - (B) perseverance
   - (C) destiny
   - (D) proportion

2. Before beginning his project, Tomas _____ what it would look like when it was completed.
   - (F) envisioned
   - (G) maneuvered
   - (H) resisted
   - (I) appealed

3. Fidelia saved a space for Jennifer at the lunch table as a _____ of friendship.
   - (A) proportion
   - (B) scholar
   - (C) gesture
   - (D) destiny

4. Kabira played several different sports, but her sister _____ in tennis.
   - (F) envisioned
   - (G) maneuvered
   - (H) specialized
   - (I) encountered

Robust Vocabulary

85

5. Marcos learned that many _____ had written books about his favorite scientist.

   (A) scholars

   (B) revelers

   (C) gestures

   (D) mavens

6. While traveling outdoors during a rainstorm, Joel wore a jacket that _____ water.

   (F) envisioned

   (G) specialized

   (H) resisted

   (I) appealed

TOTAL SCORE: _____ /6

© Harcourt • Grade 5

Grammar: Clauses and Phrases; Complex Sentences

▶ **Choose the best answer for each question.**

1. Which of the following is a dependent clause?

   Ⓐ the warm sand beneath their toes felt good

   Ⓑ before Emily picked up her shoes

   Ⓒ the waves had washed away her sand castle

   Ⓓ we met at the beach near the pier

2. Which of the following is a complex sentence?

   Ⓕ Mr. Sparks walked through the park.

   Ⓖ When Mr. Sparks walked through the park.

   Ⓗ While he walked through the park, Mr. Sparks met a friend.

   Ⓘ Mr. Sparks walked through the park and met a friend.

3. Read the following sentence.

   Because I've already seen the movie, _____.

   Which clause correctly completes the sentence?

   Ⓐ after I went to see it with Pamela.

   Ⓑ the first weekend it was showing.

   Ⓒ when I go to the bookstore.

   Ⓓ I will go to the bookstore instead.

4. Read the following sentence.

   After dinner, I will play a board game with my brother _____.

   Which clause correctly finishes the sentence?

   Ⓕ he goes to bed an hour later than I do.

   Ⓖ my favorite game is checkers.

   Ⓗ if there is enough time before bedtime.

   Ⓘ when my favorite game is checkers.

Oral Reading Fluency

The Nile River, located in Africa, is the longest river in the world, coursing for more than 4,000 miles. It flows from south to north, running from its sources all the way to the Mediterranean Sea.

There are actually three Nile Rivers in Africa. The White Nile and the Blue Nile start at different points, but they come together to form one large, powerful river.

This river is very important because it runs through a huge desert with little water, and many animals and people depend on the river to survive. The people who live along its banks eat its fish and use its waters to grow food on their farms.

Before 1968, the river often flooded, and its waters ran far over the Nile River's banks. The floods occurred after long periods of heavy rain and brought water to the farmland along the river. The floods also left behind rich dirt that was beneficial for growing crops.

Early on, people did not know where the Nile River originated. Many brave explorers tried to discover this by following the river along its banks. Because the river's course was unpredictable, it took a long time to finally reach where the river began. The journey was also difficult because of the river's fast-moving water and waterfalls. Over time, people explored the Nile in its entirety and solved this great mystery.

© Harcourt • Grade 5

Name _____

Selection Comprehension

▶ **Choose the best answer for each question.**

1. The part of the narrator is used MAINLY to
   (A) list all the characters that are in the Readers' Theater.
   (B) tell about actors' movements and expressions.
   (C) announce the start of a new scene.
   (D) tell the lines the actors are to say.

2. Which word BEST describes Chef Rudy at the beginning of "The Secret Ingredient"?
   (F) curious
   (G) playful
   (H) shrewd
   (I) proud

3. What is the MAIN problem in "The Secret Ingredient"?
   (A) Chef Rudy thinks his chili can be made only one way.
   (B) Chef Rudy wishes he could have his own cooking show.
   (C) Marco and Jessica want to help Chef Rudy cook chili.
   (D) Debbie is afraid that the show will be a total failure.

4. What happens RIGHT AFTER Chef Rudy adds the chili peppers to the pot?
   (F) Debbie helps cook the meat and the onions.
   (G) Marco says they couldn't find one ingredient.
   (H) Chef Rudy realizes an important ingredient is missing.
   (I) Chef Rudy insists that his new chili is better than ever.

5. What is the setting of "The Secret Ingredient"?
   (A) a school classroom
   (B) a television studio
   (C) an outdoor garden
   (D) a store in Mexico

6. What is one theme found in "The Secret Ingredient"?

    (F) Things that begin poorly can end well.

    (G) Too many cooks will spoil the meal.

    (H) A poor excuse is better than none at all.

    (I) A good plan is the foundation of success.

7. What is Chef Rudy MOST LIKELY to do the next time he prepares food before an audience?

    (A) call Elisa and ask for more fresh vegetables

    (B) change his favorite recipes as he is cooking

    (C) try a different ingredient in his chili recipe

    (D) let other people help him solve problems

8. In "The Secret Ingredient," both of Debbie's commercial breaks come immediately after

    (F) a sudden change in mood.

    (G) the arrival of new ingredients.

    (H) an extra demand from Chef Rudy.

    (I) an exclamation from the audience.

Written Response

9. How does Chef Rudy change in "The Secret Ingredient"? Use details to support your answer.

_____

_____

_____

_____

_____

TOTAL SCORE: _____ /8 + _____ /2

Name _____

Robust Vocabulary

▶ **Choose the best word to complete each sentence.**

1. After they argued, Christopher made _____ with his sister by helping her with her chores.
   - (A) amends
   - (B) concoctions
   - (C) scholars
   - (D) proportions

2. In the cold winter weather, Mahala's thin jacket was _____.
   - (F) irresistible
   - (G) eminent
   - (H) dismayed
   - (I) inadequate

3. The audience was eager to hear the _____ author read from her award-winning book.
   - (A) disgruntled
   - (B) eminent
   - (C) inadequate
   - (D) aghast

4. For dinner, Ethan's grandfather made a delicious _____ of beans, rice, and spices.
   - (F) charity
   - (G) gesture
   - (H) concoction
   - (I) destiny

5. Every year the school raised money for a _____ that helped local people in need.
   - (A) ruckus
   - (B) concoction
   - (C) crisis
   - (D) charity

Robust Vocabulary

91

6. When the dog chewed on Amir's new athletic shoes, Amir
   was _____.
   (F) inadequate
   (G) eminent
   (H) disgruntled
   (I) modest

7. That day, Julie was so _____ that she forgot to bring her
   book bag to school.
   (A) modest
   (B) eminent
   (C) absentminded
   (D) outlandish

8. When he dropped the freshly baked cake on the floor, the
   chef looked _____.
   (F) aghast
   (G) eminent
   (H) raspy
   (I) assured

9. Burt kept his award a secret because he was _____.
   (A) eminent
   (B) modest
   (C) aghast
   (D) irresistible

10. When Chyou couldn't find her homework, she was _____.
    (F) modest
    (G) eminent
    (H) crucial
    (I) dismayed

Robust Vocabulary

TOTAL SCORE: _____ /10

© Harcourt • Grade 5

Selection Comprehension

▶ **Choose the best answer for each question.**

1. What is the MOST LIKELY reason Miss Shipman makes the children go to school during the bad storm?
   - Ⓐ to prepare them for their next test
   - Ⓑ to prove that she is a good teacher
   - Ⓒ to make up other days they have missed
   - Ⓓ to take their minds off the rough weather

2. How is school on the ship DIFFERENT from school on land?
   - Ⓕ The children have very few books to read.
   - Ⓖ The children study six days and have no recesses.
   - Ⓗ The children learn only reading and mathematics.
   - Ⓘ The children play outside even in stormy weather.

3. Why isn't Miss Shipman good at teaching geography?
   - Ⓐ She has trouble saying the names of countries.
   - Ⓑ She has traveled less than the children have.
   - Ⓒ She does not have many good maps.
   - Ⓓ She finds the subject confusing.

4. Which word BEST describes father?
   - Ⓕ amusing
   - Ⓖ playful
   - Ⓗ brave
   - Ⓘ honest

5. Why does the author write "It was like riding a roller coaster"?
   - Ⓐ to prove that it is easy to get seasick
   - Ⓑ to tell about an ordinary day on the ship
   - Ⓒ to explain how the children like to slide on the floor
   - Ⓓ to show how the ship is going up and down on the waves

6. What can you tell about Mother?

(F) She likes smelling salt air.

(G) She grew up on a sailing ship.

(H) She plans ahead for their trips.

(I) She would rather live on the land.

7. What is the MOST LIKELY reason the family is happy at the end of the narrative?

(A) They like the music that the crew sings.

(B) They have many good things to eat.

(C) They are dressed in party clothes.

(D) They are safe on board ship.

8. How do you know that "Sailing Home" is historical fiction?

(F) The events could have happened in the past.

(G) The story exaggerates the strengths of a hero.

(H) The main character must overcome a challenge.

(I) The plot has a beginning, a middle, and an ending.

Written Response

9. Would you like to live on a ship like the one in "Sailing Home"? Use details from the story to explain why you would or would not like to live there.

_____

_____

_____

_____

Name _____

Focus Skill: Compare and Contrast

▶ Read the passage. Then choose the best answer for each question.

Spring Fever

"Good morning, everyone," said Miss Dawkins. "We are going to get started on the presentations right away, so we have time for everyone to present." Miss Dawkins's class had been working on their spring projects for the past three weeks. Each student would describe what he or she liked best about the season, spring. Kendra went first.

Kendra walked to the front of the room and set up her poster, which had "Flowers" written across the top in large, colorful letters. It was decorated with many varieties of flowers. Kendra explained that her favorite part of spring was when the flowers in her grandfather's garden began to bloom. To finish her presentation, Kendra gave each student a flower that she had designed from pipe cleaners and tissue paper.

Baxter went next, and he also set up a poster in the front of the room. Like Kendra's, Baxter's poster had one word in large letters. However, instead of "Flowers," it had "Baseball" written on it. Baxter loved playing and watching baseball. Unlike Kendra, Baxter did not hand out anything to the other students. Instead, he ended his presentation with a short video of a baseball game.

After all of the presentations, Miss Dawkins said, "You all have done excellent work. You have shown me many different reasons to anticipate spring. I can't wait for winter to be over. I must have spring fever!"

1. Which sentence from the story makes a comparison?
   Ⓐ "Each student would describe what he or she liked best about the season."
   Ⓑ "Like Kendra's, Baxter's poster had one word in large letters."
   Ⓒ "Baxter loved playing and watching baseball."
   Ⓓ "Instead, he ended his presentation with a short video of a baseball game."

© Harcourt • Grade 5

2. Which sentence from the story makes a contrast?

F "It was decorated with many varieties of flowers."

G "To finish her presentation, Kendra gave each student a flower that she had designed from pipe cleaners and tissue paper."

H "Baxter went next, and he also set up a poster in the front of the room."

I "Unlike Kendra, Baxter did not hand out anything to the other students."

3. How is Baxter's poster similar to Kendra's poster?

A Both display a variety of spring flowers.

B Both display large, colorful letters.

C Both have each student's favorite word describing spring.

D Both have the word *Baseball* at the top.

4. How is Kendra's presentation different from Baxter's presentation?

F Kendra gives flowers to each student.

G Kendra shows a video about flowers.

H Kendra explains what she enjoys about spring.

I Kendra sets up a chart at the front of the room.

Make Generalizations

▶ **Read the passage. Then choose the best answer for each question.**

A Special Day

Today, everyone in Amelia's family was busily scurrying around. Her parents had been toiling in the kitchen since early that morning, chopping, steaming, baking, and frying the family's favorite foods. Her older brothers, Diego and Paco, were outside mowing and raking the backyard for their guests, who would arrive later in the day. Amelia's job was to decorate and set the table for dinner, a job she looked forward to doing.

Amelia knew that she had to finish her homework first. She took her backpack to her room, arranged her schoolbooks on the desk, and closed the door so that it was as quiet as possible. Her best friend, Rafi, always listened to music while doing homework, but Amelia required silence for her study time.

When she had finished her schoolwork, Amelia raced downstairs. She arranged the flowers in the center of the table and folded the cloth napkins to make them look like white swans. Carefully handling the plates and glasses her parents saved for special occasions, Amelia set ten places.

Amelia had just finished when her aunt, uncle, and three cousins arrived, filling the house with the sounds of talk and laughter. The family shared stories of what had happened over the past week. Amelia especially enjoyed hearing her uncle's amusing stories about his job as a teacher.

As usual, Amelia's father served their guests first. Then, everyone joined hands as Amelia's mother told them how thankful she was that they could all be together. Amelia felt extremely fortunate to be part of such a special family gathering.

© Harcourt • Grade 5

1. Which generalization can you make from the first paragraph of the story?

    Ⓐ Children often have close friendships with their brothers and sisters.

    Ⓑ Children do not usually want to do chores when they are at home.

    Ⓒ A difficult task is easier when it is divided among several people.

    Ⓓ A difficult task is easier when one person does most of the work.

2. Read this sentence from the story.

    Her best friend, Rafi, always listened to music while doing homework, but Amelia required silence for her study time.

    Which generalization can you make from this sentence?

    Ⓕ Students try to avoid homework.

    Ⓖ Students like to listen to music.

    Ⓗ People need quiet in order to study.

    Ⓘ People learn best in different ways.

3. Read this sentence from the story.

    Amelia knew that she had to finish her homework first.

    Which is the best generalization to make about Amelia from this sentence?

    Ⓐ She avoids doing her chores.

    Ⓑ She takes her schoolwork seriously.

    Ⓒ She needs help with her homework.

    Ⓓ She ignores others in her family.

4. Which generalization can you make about the family from the last two paragraphs of the story?

    Ⓕ The family members enjoy spending time together.

    Ⓖ The family members teach one another important lessons.

    Ⓗ The family members often go out to eat dinner.

    Ⓘ The family members often find time to be alone.

Make Generalizations

98

TOTAL SCORE: _____ /4

Name _____

Robust Vocabulary

▶ **Choose the best word to complete each sentence.**

1. During the outdoor games, the children were allowed to run around and be _____.
   - (A) dignified
   - (B) eminent
   - (C) rowdy
   - (D) grim

2. As they sat in a circle, the teacher _____ the lesson by reading to the students.
   - (F) dismayed
   - (G) resisted
   - (H) conducted
   - (I) broached

3. Because she was so busy during basketball season, Becky _____ saw her friends.
   - (A) eminently
   - (B) seldom
   - (C) rowdily
   - (D) modestly

4. Ramon kept his eyeglasses in a special case so that they would not _____ in his backpack.
   - (F) shatter
   - (G) broach
   - (H) resist
   - (I) appeal

Robust Vocabulary

99

5. Alma was worried when the ship _____, but then it righted itself.

    (A) conducted

    (B) envisioned

    (C) specialized

    (D) broached

6. Shane admired how _____ his brother appeared when he wore his gray wool suit.

    (F) inflammable

    (G) absentminded

    (H) dignified

    (I) rowdy

7. Peter's mother was careful not to set _____ objects too close to the campfire.

    (A) dignified

    (B) irresistible

    (C) disgruntled

    (D) inflammable

Grammar: Common and Proper Nouns

▶ **Choose the best answer for each question.**

1. Read this sentence.

   Mingo, the orange cat, snored loudly.

   Which is the common noun in the sentence?
   (A) Mingo
   (B) cat
   (C) snored
   (D) loudly

2. Read this sentence.

   The students in the room listened carefully to Mr. Gomez.

   Which is the proper noun in the sentence?
   (F) students
   (G) room
   (H) carefully
   (I) Mr. Gomez

3. Which sentence is written correctly?
   (A) Tyson's father took him and his brother Lamont to see Dr. Finch.
   (B) Tyson's Father took him and his brother lamont to see Dr. Finch.
   (C) Tyson's father took him and his brother Lamont to see dr. Finch.
   (D) Tyson's father took him and his brother lamont to see Dr. finch.

4. Which sentence is correct?
   (F) The school is located at the end of main street.
   (G) The school is located at the end of Main street.
   (H) The school is located at the end of Main Street.
   (I) The School is located at the end of Main Street.

Grammar: Common and Proper Nouns   101   TOTAL SCORE: _____ /4

© Harcourt • Grade 5

Oral Reading Fluency

"Today is the day you've been anticipating, Sonya!" Uncle Mike announced. Although Sonya had visited Uncle Mike's ranch numerous times, today she would receive her first horseback-riding lesson.

Sonya followed her uncle into the horse barn, where he stopped in front of a stall and pointed to a tall, gray horse with gentle eyes. "Mr. Pete is an excellent choice for you," Uncle Mike said. "You wait here while I go prepare the riding area."

Sonya stood outside Mr. Pete's stall and stroked his velvety nose through the evenly spaced bars. She stood almost as tall as Mr. Pete's shoulder, but his back seemed very high and far away. Sonya began to worry about whether she would be able to get up on his back.

By the time Uncle Mike returned, Sonya's worrying had made her stomach hurt. Uncle Mike threw a saddle blanket and saddle over Mr. Pete's back and tightened the saddle's straps. He helped the anxious Sonya lead the horse out into the fenced riding corral.

Pointing at a large wooden box with steps, her uncle explained, "This is a mounting block to help you get up on Mr. Pete's back." Sonya smiled as her worries disappeared. Soon she was atop Mr. Pete's back while her uncle led the horse slowly around the corral.

_____ /WCPM

© Harcourt • Grade 5

Name _____

Selection Comprehension

▶ **Choose the best answer for each question.**

1. How do you know that "Wading into Marine Biology" is nonfiction?
   - (A) There is a main character who overcomes a challenge.
   - (B) It tells the author's personal thoughts and feelings.
   - (C) There are headings, photographs, and captions.
   - (D) It has events that could not happen in real life.

2. With which statement is the author MOST LIKELY to agree?
   - (F) Mud and seawater are very messy.
   - (G) Students should visit different places.
   - (H) People should treat nature with respect.
   - (I) Marine biologists should teach children.

3. In which zone would you MOST LIKELY find barnacles?
   - (A) The Black Zone
   - (B) The Upper Zone
   - (C) The Middle Zone
   - (D) The Lower Zone

4. How are the Middle and Lower Zones ALIKE?
   - (F) They are both exposed to air every day.
   - (G) Jellyfish and marine worms live there.
   - (H) They are full of blue-green bacteria.
   - (I) Sea lettuce protects the fish there.

5. How is Cobscook Bay DIFFERENT from other bays?
   - (A) It has tides every day.
   - (B) It is quite shallow.
   - (C) It has steep sides.
   - (D) It has tide pools.

6. Why did the author write "Wading into Marine Biology"?

(F) to persuade readers to study science

(G) to warn readers about fast-rising tides

(H) to explain to readers what tide pools look like

(I) to tell readers about changeable land near the sea

7. Under which heading are you MOST LIKELY to learn why tides rise and fall?

(A) Meeting the Tidal Residents

(B) Life in the Tidal Zone

(C) Life in a Tide Pool

(D) How Tides Work

8. How can you tell that high tide is coming in?

(F) The water is colder.

(G) The fish are still.

(H) The mussels are easy to see.

(I) The seaweed floats to the top.

READ
THINK
EXPLAIN

Written Response

9. Why is living in the tidal zone dangerous for sea animals? Use details from "Wading into Marine Biology" to explain your answer.

_____

_____

_____

_____

_____

Focus Skill: Text Structure: Compare and Contrast

▶ **Read the passage. Then choose the best answer for each
question.**

Octopus or Squid?

Ocean Animals with Legs

When most people think of octopus and squid, they think of animals
with legs that live in the ocean. However, both animals have other
features in common. Both have large heads with two large eyes that
they use to see. Both squirt out a black, ink-like liquid when they are
frightened or attacked. These two animals are also very different in many
ways.

The Octopus

An octopus gets its name from its eight legs, *octo-* means "eight." Each
of its eight legs is covered with suckers, which help the octopus move and
capture prey. Octopuses like warm, tropical water and often hide among
rocks to wait for their prey to swim past. They can grow from two inches
to sixteen feet long.

The Squid

Like an octopus, a squid has eight legs that are covered with suckers.
However, it also has two additional legs that are longer than the others.
The squid uses these long legs to catch prey. Unlike an octopus, a squid
has a long body that is shaped like a tube. It moves by taking water into
its body and squirting it back out again. This process allows the squid
to move much faster than an octopus. Instead of warm water, squid
prefer cold water in the deeper parts of the ocean. Squid also differ from
octopuses in that squid can grow much larger, up to sixty feet long.

© Harcourt • Grade 5

1. Which sentence from the passage shows a contrast?

   Ⓐ "Both squirt out a black, ink-like liquid when they are frightened or attacked."

   Ⓑ "Like an octopus, a squid has eight legs that are covered with suckers."

   Ⓒ "It moves by taking water into its body and squirting it back out again."

   Ⓓ "Instead of warm water, squid prefer cold water in the deeper parts of the ocean."

2. Which heading from the passage shows a comparison?

   Ⓕ Octopus or Squid?

   Ⓖ Ocean Animals with Eight Legs

   Ⓗ The Octopus

   Ⓘ The Squid

3. How is the body of an octopus similar to the body of a squid?

   Ⓐ Both have bodies that are shaped like tubes.

   Ⓑ Both have two legs that are longer than the others.

   Ⓒ Both have two large eyes on their heads.

   Ⓓ Both can grow up to sixty feet long.

4. How is a squid different from an octopus?

   Ⓕ A squid moves by taking in water and squirting it out again.

   Ⓖ A squid squirts out a black, ink-like liquid when it is attacked.

   Ⓗ A squid has eight legs that are covered with suckers.

   Ⓘ A squid can grow from five inches to three feet long.

Expository Forms

▶ **Choose the best answer for each question.**

1. Which of the following is an expository text?
   - Ⓐ a fable
   - Ⓑ a short story
   - Ⓒ a folktale
   - Ⓓ a news article

2. Which is a characteristic of all expository texts?
   - Ⓕ They describe imaginary events.
   - Ⓖ They begin with a table of contents.
   - Ⓗ They give facts and information.
   - Ⓘ They include a chart or a diagram.

3. Which of the following is an expository text?
   - Ⓐ a book about the history of Mexico
   - Ⓑ a short story that appears in a newspaper
   - Ⓒ a song about wishing for adventure
   - Ⓓ a book about traveling in a time machine

4. Why is a set of instructions an example of an expository text?
   - Ⓕ It uses both pictures and words to describe a topic.
   - Ⓖ It gives facts and information about a topic.
   - Ⓗ It describes steps that must be followed in order.
   - Ⓘ It tells a story that includes real people or events.

5. Which is the most likely title of an expository text?
   - Ⓐ *The Adventures of Popsicle the Guinea Pig*
   - Ⓑ *Voyage to Planet Zerkon*
   - Ⓒ *The Life of Rosa Parks*
   - Ⓓ *A Child's Book of Greek Myths*

© Harcourt • Grade 5

Name _____

6. Read this passage.

Octopus or Squid?

Ocean Animals with Eight Legs

When most people think of octopus or squid, they think of animals with eight legs that live in the ocean. However, both animals have other features in common. Both have large heads, and they use their two large eyes to see. Both squirt out black, ink-like liquid when they are frightened or attacked. These two animals are also very different in many ways.

How do you know that this passage is an example of expository text?

(F) It has a title and a heading about ocean animals.

(G) It tells a story about a squid and an octopus.

(H) It uses compare and contrast text structure.

(I) It is a paragraph about eight-legged animals.

TOTAL SCORE: _____ /6

© Harcourt • Grade 5

Name _____

Make Generalizations

▶ Read the passage. Then choose the best answer for each
question.

Life in the Tundra

Imagine living in a place where the weather is almost always very
cold and where the ground remains frozen almost all year long. These
conditions are a fact of life in the large, open plains known as the tundra.
Areas of tundra exist near the North and South Poles as well as on some
high mountaintops.

In tundra areas the climate is cold and dry. These areas have extremely
short summers and long winters with little snow or rain. Periods of cold
last for so long that the ground remains frozen almost all of the time.
When it does rain, or when snow melts, water cannot drain into the
frozen ground. Instead, it stays on the surface and creates puddles and
ponds.

Few plants can survive in the tundra. Because it is very windy, plants
must be low to the ground. For this reason, the tundra has no trees and
is covered mostly with different kinds of grass and moss.

Like the plants, all animals that live in the tundra have become used
to existing in a cold climate. Certain types of deer, goats, bears, wolves,
and rabbits survive well in these areas. Because of the large amounts of
grass and standing water, the tundra is home to many mosquitoes and
grasshoppers. Birds that live in the tundra usually leave for warmer areas
before the long winter.

1. Which is the best summary of the second paragraph?
   (A) The tundra has ponds formed by rain and melted snow.
   (B) The tundra has a short summer season.
   (C) The tundra is cold and dry for most of the year.
   (D) The tundra receives little rain and snow.

Make Generalizations

© Harcourt • Grade 5

2. What generalization can you make about the second paragraph?

(F) The weather in tundra areas is going through a time of change.

(G) The weather usually makes life difficult for people in the tundra.

(H) The weather is no different in the tundra than it is in other areas.

(I) The weather in tundra areas has a powerful effect on the landscape.

3. Which is the best summary of the last paragraph?

(A) Animals in the tundra move to warmer areas in winter.

(B) Animals in the tundra have adapted to its climate.

(C) Animals in the tundra are similar to animals in other areas.

(D) Many different types of animals live in the tundra.

4. What generalization can you make about the last paragraph?

(F) Only certain types of animals can live in difficult climates.

(G) Only a few people have traveled to places like the tundra.

(H) Areas with cold weather always have plentiful animal life.

(I) Areas with little rain or snow usually have cold temperatures.

Make Generalizations

110

TOTAL SCORE: _____ /4

Name _____

Robust Vocabulary

▶ **Choose the best word to complete each sentence.**

1. When Belen moved to a new school, he had to _____ to all of the differences.
   - (A) conduct
   - (B) recoil
   - (C) shatter
   - (D) adjust

2. The horse was annoyed by the _____ fly that kept buzzing around its head.
   - (F) dignified
   - (G) resident
   - (H) pesky
   - (I) internal

3. The science class looked for interesting _____ of plants to draw in their journals.
   - (A) debris
   - (B) residents
   - (C) specimens
   - (D) scholars

4. Because she never needed to look at a map, people said Hannah's sense of direction was _____.
   - (F) internal
   - (G) inflammable
   - (H) pesky
   - (I) dignified

© Harcourt • Grade 5

Name _____

5. A person will usually _____ from the unpleasant odor of
    burning rubber.
    (A) adjust
    (B) broach
    (C) shatter
    (D) recoil

6. After the street fair, volunteers picked up cans, papers, and other _____
    and put them in trash bins.
    (F) specimens
    (G) concoctions
    (H) debris
    (I) residents

7. Some of the people in Nicole's apartment building came to welcome
    their new _____.
    (A) specimens
    (B) debris
    (C) gestures
    (D) residents

TOTAL SCORE: _____ /7

© Harcourt • Grade 5

Name _____

Grammar: Singular and Plural Nouns

▶ **Choose the best answer for each question.**

1. Which noun is singular?
   - (A) caravans
   - (B) package
   - (C) geese
   - (D) women

2. Which noun is plural?
   - (F) business
   - (G) distress
   - (H) society
   - (I) people

3. Read the sentence.

   After the shopping trip, they put all of their _____ in the trunk of the car.

   Which is the correct form of the missing word?
   - (A) purchase
   - (B) purchase's
   - (C) purchases
   - (D) purchases'

4. Read the sentence.

   You can find various large animals such as _____ in the northern forests.

   Which is the correct form of the missing word?
   - (F) moose
   - (G) moose's
   - (H) mooses
   - (I) moosses

TOTAL SCORE: _____ /4

© Harcourt • Grade 5

Name _____

Oral Reading Fluency

Andrew was excitedly looking forward to visiting his friend Renaldo. A vast pine forest surrounded Renaldo's house, and the boys had planned an exploratory hike through the woods. When Andrew arrived, he and Renaldo placed some sandwiches and bottled water into a backpack. Then they started down a path that led into the forest.

As they made their way onto the path, the atmosphere became quiet and mysterious. Huge pine trees rose far above their heads, and sunlight streamed through the branches like golden threads. The silence was broken only by the sounds of twigs snapping under their feet and a few startled birds flapping their wings. After exploring for a few hours, the boys flopped onto the ground to eat lunch. Renaldo leaned back with his hands on the ground.

"There is something hard under the dirt here," he said with surprise. "Let's see what it is!" The boys quickly brushed away pine needles and dirt and found a long, flat rock. Using sticks, the boys kept digging, and soon they had uncovered three stone steps.

"These must have been the front steps to a house!" said Andrew in astonishment. "I wonder who lived here and what happened to their house." This was a tremendous discovery for the boys, and they could not wait to tell their parents what they had found.

© Harcourt • Grade 5

Selection Comprehension

▶ **Choose the best answer for each question.**

1. What is the MOST LIKELY reason Stormy loves the ocean?
   - (A) He likes to go deep-sea fishing.
   - (B) He enjoys being in rough seas.
   - (C) He enjoys working as a cabin boy.
   - (D) He likes being in a place big enough.

2. Why do the people from Cape Cod send Stormy to Boston?
   - (F) They can no longer feed him.
   - (G) They think the city will be big like he is.
   - (H) They want him to make new friends.
   - (I) They hope he will become a sailor.

3. What is the MOST LIKELY reason Stormy decides to leave Boston?
   - (A) He decides to get a better job.
   - (B) He wants to become a farmer.
   - (C) He is lonely and has no friends.
   - (D) He misses the people on Cape Cod.

4. What is the MOST LIKELY reason why all the Yankee clipper crews want to sail with Stormy?
   - (F) They want to be on his big ship.
   - (G) They think that he can help them.
   - (H) They believe he is a good swimmer.
   - (I) They want to sing sea songs with him.

5. What is Stormy's MAIN problem in "Stormalong"?
   - (A) He has difficulty making friends.
   - (B) He wants to be a sailor on a big ship.
   - (C) He is so large he has to sleep in a rowboat.
   - (D) He feels out of place no matter where he is.

**Selection Comprehension
"Stormalong"**

© Harcourt • Grade 5

6. Why does Stormy move to the plains of Kansas?

F He wants to be where people are unfamiliar with the sea.

G He hopes to show pioneers what a big oar looks like.

H He wants to become a farmer and grow potatoes.

I He hopes to learn how to do square dancing.

7. Which idea BEST shows that Stormy is strong?

A When he scrubs the decks, the wood peels off.

B When he gets near the rail, the ship tips.

C Giant waves roll when he starts to sing.

D He is too big to sleep in a hammock.

8. How do you know that "Stormalong" is a tall tale?

F It has characters, places, and events that are real.

G It exaggerates the strength and abilities of a hero.

H It has a plot with a beginning, a middle, and an ending.

I It has stage directions so it can be performed for an audience.

Written Response

9. What is the MOST LIKELY reason Stormalong would stand alone, listening to the men sing, and gaze at the sea with a look of great sorrow? Use details from "Stormalong" to explain your answer.

_____

_____

_____

_____

_____

_____

Selection Comprehension
"Stormalong"

© Harcourt • Grade 5

116

TOTAL SCORE: _____ /8 + _____ /2

Focus Skill: Cause and Effect

▶ **Read the passage. Then choose the best answer for
each question.**

Chi's Trip

As she carried bags to the car, Jun said, "Chi, aren't you going to pack anything for the long drive? You know it can be boring." Annoyed at the interruption, Chi shook his head irritably and continued reading *The Mystery of the Missing Monkeys*. He finished the book just as his mother started the car.

Once in the car, Chi felt restless. He wished he had brought another book to read. Next to him, Jun was drawing, and her bag overflowed with fun activities. Chi knew it was too soon to ask his mother when they would reach their destination, so he shifted in his seat again. This time, he bumped into Jun, causing her to draw a jagged line across her paper.

"Chi! Stop fidgeting! You've ruined my drawing!" Jun said angrily. "I told you to pack a bag for the long drive because you get bored so quickly!" Chi nodded. He knew that his sister was right. He should have listened when she had reminded him to pack activities for the ride.

Jun reached into her bag and pulled out a new mystery book for Chi.

"Here, Chi. I planned ahead and brought this for you, but next time, take my advice, okay?" Chi gratefully accepted the book and apologized. No longer restless, Chi tackled his new book, and as he read, the trip whizzed by.

1. What causes Chi to get annoyed?
   Ⓐ His sister interrupts his reading.
   Ⓑ His mother starts the car.
   Ⓒ His sister ruins his drawing.
   Ⓓ His mother tells him to pack.

2. What effect does Chi's mistake have on Jun?
   Ⓕ She cannot concentrate on her drawing.
   Ⓖ She must loan Chi the book she is reading.
   Ⓗ Her drawing is accidentally ruined.
   Ⓘ Her book is lost during the trip.

Focus Skill: Cause and Effect

© Harcourt • Grade 5

3. What causes Jun to pack a mystery book?

   (A) She wants to read a book with her brother.

   (B) She knows that Chi will not pack a book for himself.

   (C) Her mother tells her to pack a fun book for Chi.

   (D) Her brother asks her to pack a book for him.

4. What effect does Jun's planning have on Chi?

   (F) Chi has to tell his mother that he did not pack.

   (G) Chi has to draw pictures with his sister.

   (H) Chi is angry that his sister took his book.

   (I) Chi is no longer bored on the long drive.

© Harcourt • Grade 5

Vocabulary Strategies: Using Word Parts

▶ **Choose the best answer for each question.**

1. What is the suffix in the word *honorable*?

   Ⓐ hon

   Ⓑ honor

   Ⓒ able

   Ⓓ e

2. Which is the root word of *disagreeable*?

   Ⓕ agree

   Ⓖ disagree

   Ⓗ agreeable

   Ⓘ able

3. The word *misfortune* is made up of the prefix *mis-*, meaning "ill or
   wrong," and the root word *fortune*, meaning "luck."
   What does the word *misfortune* mean?

   Ⓐ a sign of luck

   Ⓑ bad luck

   Ⓒ lucky person

   Ⓓ lucky thoughts

4. What is the prefix in the word *disappearing*?

   Ⓕ appear

   Ⓖ ing

   Ⓗ di

   Ⓘ dis

Vocabulary Strategies: Using Word Parts

Name _____

5. The word *warily* is made up of the root word *wary*, meaning
    "careful," and the suffix *-ly*, meaning "in a certain way."
    What does the word *warily* mean?

    (A) caring for yourself

    (B) in a careful manner

    (C) caring about others

    (D) a way of being careless

6. Read this sentence

    > Although my friend was *ungracious* when I offered
    > her part of my snack, I still shared it with her.

    What does the word *ungracious* mean?

    (F) full of grace

    (G) without grace

    (H) the act of being gracious

    (I) graciousness

TOTAL SCORE: _____ /6

© Harcourt • Grade 5

Make Generalizations

▶ Read the passage. Then choose the best answer for
each question.

Orion Learns a Lesson

One sun-drenched afternoon, Randy's mother suggested he take his
younger brother, Orion, to the playground located next to their house.
Orion had just celebrated his third birthday, and he was delighted to be
spending time with his older brother.

When they arrived at the playground, Orion scampered over to the
swings. Then he held on to the two chains with two chubby fists, jumped
up, and pulled himself onto the seat of the swing on his first try.

"Look! I got up all by myself!" Orion shouted gleefully. Randy came
over to push Orion on the swing, because Orion's short legs could not
reach the ground. Randy showed Orion how to keep himself going by
pumping his legs back and forth in the air. After a few minutes, Orion
wanted to get down from the swing. He sprinted over to the slide, arriving
at the ladder just behind another boy about his age.

Orion grabbed on to the rungs of the ladder, pulling the other boy out
of the way. As he began to climb, he called out for Randy to watch him.
Randy ran over and gently pulled Orion off the ladder. Then, Randy told
the other little boy that he could use the slide first.

"Orion, I know you are excited to be here with me," Randy said, "but
you have to share the playground equipment with the other children here.
That way, everybody can have a good time, and you might even make
new friends." Then, Orion and the other boy took turns on the slide
while Randy clapped and cheered enthusiastically.

1. What generalization can you make about Orion's actions on the
   swings?

   (A) Young children usually enjoy playing with other children their
   own age.

   (B) Young children spend too little time with their brothers and
   sisters.

   (C) Young children are proud when they can do things by themselves.

   (D) Young children often copy the actions of older people they know.

© Harcourt • Grade 5

Name _____

2. What generalization can you make about Randy pushing Orion on the swing?

   Ⓕ Some children learn a new skill best by watching others.

   Ⓖ People can learn to enjoy things they dislike at first.

   Ⓗ Some children dislike being the center of attention.

   Ⓘ People often take opportunities to teach children new things.

3. What generalization can you make about Orion pulling the other boy out of the way?

   Ⓐ Young children always forget their manners on the playground.

   Ⓑ Young children can get overly excited and need to be shown how to be fair.

   Ⓒ Young children behave the way their brothers and sisters behave.

   Ⓓ Young children dislike playing with other children their age.

4. What generalization can you make about Randy allowing the other boy to use the slide?

   Ⓕ Older children can model good behavior for their younger brothers or sisters.

   Ⓖ Young children usually behave best when they play with older children.

   Ⓗ Older children usually enjoy being responsible for younger children.

   Ⓘ Young children fully understand why they must share and take turns.

Make Generalizations

122

TOTAL SCORE: _____ /4

Robust Vocabulary

► **Choose the best word to complete each sentence.**

1. In autumn, the flowers that bloomed in the summer become dry
   and _____.
   - (A) adjusted
   - (B) withered
   - (C) betrayed
   - (D) recoiled

2. Before Lei found a group of good friends, she felt like an _____ at
   her new school.
   - (F) internal
   - (G) adjuster
   - (H) outcast
   - (I) escapade

3. On their trip, Anya and Dimitri met interesting people and had plenty
   of exciting _____.
   - (A) escapades
   - (B) residents
   - (C) specimens
   - (D) yearnings

4. Over the years, Mr. Denton earned a _____ for being the best
   teacher in the school.
   - (F) specimen
   - (G) reputation
   - (H) bellow
   - (I) resident

© Harcourt • Grade 5

Name _____

5. Shane could hear his mother _____ his name all the way from the backyard.

   (A) broaching
   (B) yearning
   (C) recoiling
   (D) bellowing

6. When her brother read her diary marked "secret," Juanita felt _____.

   (F) adjusted
   (G) dignified
   (H) betrayed
   (I) withered

7. Because they were written in another language, the books were _____ to Julian.

   (A) withered
   (B) internal
   (C) inflammable
   (D) unfathomable

8. When he looked at pictures of the Grand Canyon, Tim felt a strong _____ to visit it.

   (F) shattering
   (G) reputation
   (H) yearning
   (I) recoiling

Name _____

Grammar: Possessive Nouns

▶ **Choose the best answer for each question.**

1. Which word replaces the phrase *belonging to Jordan*?
   - (A) Jordan's
   - (B) Jordans
   - (C) Jordans's
   - (D) Jordan

2. What is the possessive form of the noun *Thomas*?
   - (F) Thoma's
   - (G) Thomase's
   - (H) Thomas'
   - (I) Thomas's

3. Which sentence uses a possessive noun correctly?
   - (A) The neighbors cat ran in my house.
   - (B) Our school principals' secretary called a meeting.
   - (C) A monorail's track is above ground.
   - (D) We went to our schools's library after class.

4. Which possessive form replaces the phrase *owned by artists*?
   - (F) artists's
   - (G) artists'
   - (H) artist's
   - (I) artists

TOTAL SCORE: _____ /4

© Harcourt • Grade 5

Oral Reading Fluency

The tree sloth is a unique and unusual animal that lives in South America and Central America. Only two kinds of sloths exist today. One has two long toes on each front leg. The other has three toes on each front leg. Both sloth species spend most of their lives in the trees of tropical forests. They eat leaves and shoots from trees.

One trait that makes sloths so unusual is that they spend almost their entire lives hanging upside down from the branches of trees. They have strong legs with long, curved claws. Their legs help them suspend from trees while they eat, sleep, and even give birth to their young. Sloths usually come down from trees only once a week. Therefore, it is difficult for sloths to travel on the ground because they spend so much time hanging from trees.

Another unusual trait of sloths is their lack of speed. They are among the slowest animals in nature. They move one leg at a time, and they move very carefully. This makes sloths easy prey. However, when sloths lie still or sleep, it is much easier for them to stay hidden from their enemies, such as jaguars. Furthermore, their green fur blends in with the colors of the trees and helps them hide.

Name _____

Selection Comprehension

▶ **Choose the best answer for each question.**

1. How do you know "A Drop of Water" is nonfiction?
   (A) It has a problem that readers must solve.
   (B) It tells what a group of people believed in the past.
   (C) It has headings that begin sections of related information.
   (D) It is a story about exaggerated or impossible happenings.

2. Which of these facts would be MOST important to include in a summary of "A Drop of Water"?
   (F) A steel pin can "float" on water.
   (G) Water cycles are hard to control.
   (H) Steam is very hot water vapor.
   (I) Water can be a liquid, a solid, or a gas.

3. Surface tension helps the tiny parts of a drop of water to
   (A) hold together.
   (B) form strands.
   (C) cling to glass.
   (D) change to a vapor.

4. Water needs heat in order to
   (F) stick to surfaces.
   (G) stay in liquid form.
   (H) lock its parts together.
   (I) make six-sided designs.

5. Which of these is the result of water changing from a gas to a solid?
   (A) rain
   (B) dew
   (C) frost
   (D) drops

6. Under which heading are you MOST LIKELY to learn about the way water evaporates?

    (F) Ice

    (G) Water Vapor

    (H) Water's Elastic Surface

    (I) Condensation

7. Why did the author write "A Drop of Water"?

    (A) to tell what happens when water freezes

    (B) to explain how water changes and moves

    (C) to persuade readers to protect our water supply

    (D) to show what would happen in a world without water

8. Which would MOST help someone understand the ideas in "A Drop of Water"?

    (F) watching experiments that make water change forms

    (G) looking at snowflakes swirling during a storm

    (H) looking at frost patterns formed on a window

    (I) watching water as it flows from a faucet

READ THINK EXPLAIN

Written Response

9. **COMPARING TEXTS** How can different forms of water be used? Use details from "A Drop of Water," "Rain, Dance!", "Steam," and "Ice Cycle" to explain your answer.

_____

_____

_____

_____

Focus Skill: Text Structure: Cause and Effect

▶ Read the passage. Then choose the best answer for each question.

Nimah Goes to New York

One morning Nimah came across a newspaper lying open on the kitchen table. As she glanced at it, she saw a picture of a very tall and impressive building in New York City called the Empire State Building. She read an article about how many people travel from all over the world to stand on the roof of this building. From there, they admire the magnificent view of New York City.

After reading the article, Nimah went outside to her backyard. As she stood on the grass alongside the patio, she had an idea, and she began gathering rocks, sticks, and buckets full of sand. When two hours had gone by, Nimah's father became concerned, so he went outside to look for her.

"Look, Father," said Nimah, "this is the Empire State Building. Would you like to come for a visit?" Nimah had built a model of the famous building, and her father was very impressed. He called for Nimah's brother, sister, and grandparents to come see what she had made.

When Nimah's grandmother saw the model of the Empire State Building that Nimah had built, she told her how she had visited New York City on her twelfth birthday. She told Nimah how different the city was back then. Soon, several of Nimah's neighbors joined the group in the backyard. Before long, the adults were sharing stories about New York City. Finally, Nimah's father offered to prepare dinner for the entire group of friends and neighbors.

When Nimah went to bed that night, she enthusiastically scribbled in her journal. *Today I visited New York City*, she wrote, *but I didn't leave my own backyard!*

1. What causes Nimah to first learn about the Empire State Building?
   - (A) She sees the building in a movie about New York City.
   - (B) She studies the building as a part of a project for school.
   - (C) She hears stories about New York City from family and friends.
   - (D) She finds a newspaper article about it on her kitchen table.

2. What effect does the newspaper article have on Nimah?

(F) It makes her ask her father to take her to New York City.

(G) It makes her want to read more about New York City.

(H) It gives her the idea to create a model of the building in her backyard.

(I) It gives her the idea to ask her grandmother about New York City.

3. What causes Nimah's father to go looking for her?

(A) He needs to tell her that he is having people over for dinner.

(B) He is worried because he hasn't seen her for two hours.

(C) He wants to see how her model building is coming along.

(D) He wants to show her the article from the newspaper.

4. What effect does Nimah's model have on her family and neighbors?

(F) It makes them want to share their stories about New York City.

(G) It makes them want to help her create models of other buildings.

(H) It makes them decide to invite more people over for dinner.

(I) It makes them decide to plan a vacation to New York City.

Name _____

Vocabulary Strategies: Using Word Parts

▶ **Choose the best answer for each question.**

1. Which root word is part of the word *abbreviation*?

  Ⓐ brev

  Ⓑ rev

  Ⓒ viat

  Ⓓ tion

2. Read this sentence.

> My aunt's *unavoidable* accident caused her to have to stay
> in bed for the day.

What is the prefix in the word *unavoidable*?

  Ⓕ avoid

  Ⓖ avoidable

  Ⓗ able

  Ⓘ un

3. Read this sentence.

> The video we watched was boring and *unremarkable*.

What is the suffix in the word *unremarkable*?

  Ⓐ un

  Ⓑ able

  Ⓒ remark

  Ⓓ remarkable

© Harcourt • Grade 5

4. The word *observable* is made up of the root word *observe*, meaning "to notice," and the suffix *-able*.
What does the word *observable* mean?

(F) not noticed

(G) able to be noticed

(H) the state of noticing

(I) was noticed

5. Which word does not have a prefix?

(A) unnoticed

(B) beneath

(C) reconstruct

(D) discharge

6. The word *clumsiness* is made up of the root word *clumsy*, meaning "awkward," and the suffix *-ness*.
What does the word *clumsiness* mean?

(F) was awkward

(G) not awkward

(H) able to be awkward

(I) the state of being awkward

Name _____

Expository Forms

▶ Read the passage. Then choose the best answer for
each question.

Why Do Leaves Change Color?

Where Leaf Colors Come From

If you live in a place where the leaves change color in autumn, you
probably notice that only some trees become colorful. The trees that
change color have special types of leaves that contain the building blocks
for two colors. The first color is green, the color of the leaves during
spring and summer. The second color can be red, orange, yellow, or
brown, which are the colors that are visible in autumn. Both colors are
inside each leaf all year long, but in spring and summer the green color
forms the top layer.

1. What is the purpose of this passage?
   A to describe different leaf characters in a story
   B to entertain people with a story about leaves
   C to explain where the color of leaves come from
   D to persuade people to rake their leaves

2. How do you know the passage is an expository text?
   F It has a passage title.
   G It provides information about a subject.
   H It uses humor about leaves.
   I It has a main idea and details.

© Harcourt • Grade 5

3. Which of the following is most likely to be an expository text?

   (A) text with dialogue between characters

   (B) text that tells a myth

   (C) text that tells you how to do something

   (D) text that has make-believe characters

4. Which of the following features would you most likely find in an expository text?

   (F) a diagram

   (G) stage directions

   (H) verses and stanzas

   (I) painted drawings

Name _____

Robust Vocabulary

▶ **Choose the best word to complete each sentence.**

1. After Kofi left the room, his dog made Kofi's sandwich _____.
   - (A) shatter
   - (B) accumulate
   - (C) recoil
   - (D) vanish

2. After each art class, the box of drawing paper was empty and needed _____.
   - (F) underlying
   - (G) yearning
   - (H) replenishing
   - (I) broaching

3. At the fair, one fun house mirror makes your body look shorter and the next _____ your body.
   - (A) accumulates
   - (B) elongates
   - (C) yearns
   - (D) broaches

4. During the storm, Alejandro wondered how much snow would finally _____ in his yard.
   - (F) wither
   - (G) accumulate
   - (H) vanish
   - (I) conduct

5. The soldiers standing at attention in front of the palace were so _____ that I thought they were statues.
   - (A) rigid
   - (B) adjusted
   - (C) elastic
   - (D) rowdy

Robust Vocabulary

135

6. Ms. Martin was sewing a pair of pants with an _____
   waistband so they would be easier to put on.

   F intricate

   G elongated

   H elastic

   I internal

7. Taina loved watching the builders erect the _____ beams that would
   support the house.

   A unfathomable

   B replenishing

   C dignified

   D underlying

8. Because Mercedes had a mind for details, she understood the _____
   workings of computers.

   F withered

   G elastic

   H intricate

   I rigid

Grammar: Pronouns and Antecedents

▶ **Choose the best answer for each question.**

1. Read this sentence.

   In the play, the actor was the star of the show.

   Which pronoun replaces the noun *the actor*?

   (A) it

   (B) he

   (C) they

   (D) we

2. Which of the following correctly completes the second sentence?

   Micky can cast only one vote in the election.
   After voting once, _____ must go home.

   (F) him

   (G) he

   (H) they

   (I) it

3. Read these sentences.

   Ramona wrote a poem for her mother. Then, she drew a picture.

   Which noun does the pronoun *she* refer to?

   (A) mother

   (B) picture

   (C) poem

   (D) Ramona

4. Read these sentences.

   Jesse and Manuel helped prepare dinner. They made the salad.

   Which noun(s) does the pronoun *they* refer to?

   (F) Jesse and Manuel

   (G) father

   (H) dinner

   (I) salad

Grammar: Pronouns and Antecedents   137 | TOTAL SCORE: _____ /4 |

© Harcourt • Grade 5

Oral Reading Fluency

Although penguins are birds, they do not have the ability to fly. Penguins live in some of the coldest locations on earth. However, they have a thick layer of fat that helps keep them warm in these extremely cold temperatures.

Penguins spend most of their time swimming in cold waters, looking for food. A penguin's strong flippers and smooth, sleek body makes it an excellent swimmer. Penguins steer with their legs and use their flippers as paddles. Their feathers fit tightly together in order to keep their bodies warm. Staying at sea for weeks at a time, groups of penguins use their special features to feed on fish and other small sea creatures in the cold ocean water.

There are seventeen types of penguins, and most reside around frigid ice and freezing snow. They usually live in colonies together with other penguins of their kind. Penguins range in size from the little blue penguin, which is about one foot tall, to the emperor penguin, which stands at almost four feet. You can tell penguins apart by the various patterns on their heads and necks, but most have black backs and white bellies. Their coloring helps camouflage them in the water.

Penguins are unique animals that have adapted to one of the harshest environments in the world. They use their special skills to thrive in a dangerous climate.

© Harcourt • Grade 5

Name _____

Selection Comprehension

▶ **Choose the best answer for each question.**

1. The author wrote "How Prairie Became Ocean" MAINLY to
   - (A) describe how the Yuroks used to live.
   - (B) show what Yurok children did for fun.
   - (C) explain how the Yuroks hunted game and fish.
   - (D) tell what the Yuroks used to believe about nature.

2. Why doesn't Thunder like the prairie?
   - (F) It contains no life.
   - (G) There are no clouds.
   - (H) It is boring to look at.
   - (I) There are no mountains.

3. Grandmother says Kingfisher was "swift as the wind" in order to help the children
   - (A) know how Kingfisher sounded.
   - (B) imagine how Kingfisher moved.
   - (C) picture what Kingfisher looked like.
   - (D) understand what Kingfisher thought.

4. How do you know the events in "How Prairie Became Ocean" couldn't happen in real life?
   - (F) A bird could not fly several miles away.
   - (G) Mussels and clams could not live in tide pools.
   - (H) Thunder and Earthquake could not talk.
   - (I) Salmon and whales could not swim in the ocean.

5. What is the MAIN reason the ocean is important to the children?
   - (A) It makes a lot of noise during a storm.
   - (B) It provides both beauty and food.
   - (C) It prevents them from sleeping.
   - (D) It is prettier than a flat prairie.

6. In this Readers' Theater, the chorus represents

(F) Earthquake.

(G) Kingfisher.

(H) Thunder.

(I) Yurok children.

7. Why does Grandmother tell about Thunder and Earthquake?

(A) to warn that storms can be dangerous

(B) to prove that she is a good storyteller

(C) to calm everyone during the storm

(D) to present a quick science lesson

8. Why do Thunder and Earthquake want to stay in the new land?

(F) They think the land is now a beautiful place.

(G) They worked hard making the land look better.

(H) They want to stay to be honored for their efforts.

(I) They want Kingfisher to know where to find them.

READ THINK EXPLAIN

Written Response

9. Which character—Thunder, Earthquake, or Kingfisher—do you think was MOST important in changing the prairie into an ocean? Use details from "How Prairie Became Ocean" to support your answer.

_____

_____

_____

_____

Name _____

Robust Vocabulary

▶ **Choose the best word to complete each sentence.**

1. Hiking to the top of the mountain was a challenging _____.
   (A) recount
   (B) specimen
   (C) outcast
   (D) endeavor

2. After playing outside on a hot day, Kyle's throat felt _____.
   (F) betrayed
   (G) parched
   (H) uninhabitable
   (I) monotonous

3. During the long winter, farm families could _____ themselves with canned or dried foods.
   (A) vanish
   (B) sustain
   (C) recount
   (D) adjust

4. The child fell asleep as her brother read in a _____ voice.
   (F) teeming
   (G) brimming
   (H) monotonous
   (I) bellowing

5. Liv's aunt would often _____ fun stories from her childhood.
   (A) recount
   (B) recoil
   (C) sustain
   (D) vanish

Robust Vocabulary

© Harcourt • Grade 5

6. Cullen walked carefully so as not to spill the cups that were _____ with juice.

(F) brimming

(G) replenishing

(H) teeming

(I) yearning

7. Sad events made Rob's story a _____ tale.

(A) parched

(B) sorrowful

(C) uninhabitable

(D) vanish

8. Ian wished he could live in the tree house, but he knew it was _____.

(F) sorrowful

(G) monotonous

(H) uninhabitable

(I) inflammable

9. On the first day of the sale, the store was _____ with shoppers.

(A) sorrowful

(B) bellowing

(C) teeming

(D) underlying

10. Dante was so nervous about the trip that he continued to _____ on it.

(F) sustain

(G) vanish

(H) recount

(I) dwell

Robust Vocabulary

142

TOTAL SCORE: _____ /10

Name _____

Selection Comprehension

▶ **Choose the best answer for each question.**

1. Which word BEST describes Zoe?
   - (A) suspicious
   - (B) cautious
   - (C) clever
   - (D) timid

2. How are Zoe and Natalie ALIKE?
   - (F) Both act as an agent.
   - (G) Both write left-handed.
   - (H) Both have a secret plan.
   - (I) Both get a book published.

3. Why does Mrs. Clayton feel "choked up" when Natalie hands her an Advance Reader's Copy?
   - (A) She wants to read the book.
   - (B) She is pleased that her student succeeded.
   - (C) She is worried that Natalie will not sell many books.
   - (D) She thinks she will never get a real copy of the book.

4. Which detail would be MOST important to include in a summary of the story?
   - (F) Natalie has Zoe copy over her comments.
   - (G) There are only two errors on the fourth manuscript.
   - (H) Natalie's mother is the editor of her daughter's book.
   - (I) The Advance Reader's Copy is printed on thin paper.

5. What is the MAIN reason Zoe avoids telling Natalie about the party?
   - (A) She knows that Letha will be angry.
   - (B) She is certain that Natalie will not go.
   - (C) She wants Mrs. Nelson to tell Natalie.
   - (D) She wants credit for making it a surprise.

**Selection Comprehension
"The School Story"**

© Harcourt • Grade 5

6. Which action BEST shows that Hannah is nervous about the party?

(F) She reads the review to Tom Morton.

(G) She worries that Letha might be angry.

(H) She makes sure that a big banner is made.

(I) She goes to the conference room three times.

7. How do you know that "A School Story" is realistic fiction?

(A) The story characters have feelings that real people have.

(B) The story is the author's account of his or her own life.

(C) The story provides facts and details about a topic.

(D) The characters are actual historical figures.

8. Why does the author write that Zoe "headed straight toward Hannah Nelson like a locomotive"?

(F) to show that nothing can stop her

(G) to show that she is big and strong

(H) to show that she makes a lot of noise

(I) to show that she is on a time schedule

Written Response

9. How are Zoe and Natalie DIFFERENT? Use details from "A School Story" to support your answer.

_____

_____

_____

_____

_____

Focus Skill: Make Inferences

▶ Read the passage. Then choose the best answer for each question.

The Costume Contest

"Janelle!" said Kenyatta excitedly. "Next weekend is the Colonial Times festival, and my aunt told me that she would help us make outfits for the costume contest!"

Janelle was silent as Kenyatta ran into the next room to get paper and colored pencils. Kenyatta handed half of the supplies to Janelle and started drawing a picture of a colonial dress. It had a large skirt with layers, long sleeves, and ribbons that laced all the way down the back. Janelle felt a knot in her stomach as she imagined herself wearing that costume in front of all of the people at the festival.

"Kenyatta," Janelle said, "I don't want to go to the festival. I think it would be more fun just to stay home."

Kenyatta looked stunned. "How could staying home be more fun than going to the festival?" she asked. "We're going to have the best costumes of anyone there, and we might even win a prize!"

Janelle realized how strange her words sounded as she listened to Kenyatta repeat them, and she decided to tell her friend the truth. When she was finished, Kenyatta smiled.

"Janelle, you don't have to wear an outfit like mine. You can design any kind of colonial-period costume you like!" Janelle felt relieved, and wondered why she had gotten so nervous. She grabbed a colored pencil and began making a drawing of the costume she knew would win first prize.

1. Why is Janelle silent as Kenyatta gets paper and pencils?
   (A) Janelle feels tired and wants to return home.
   (B) Janelle thinks that Kenyatta's idea is boring.
   (C) Janelle is not excited about the costume contest.
   (D) Janelle and Kenyatta have just been arguing.

Focus Skill: Make Inferences

© Harcourt • Grade 5

2. Why does Janelle feel a knot in her stomach?

(F) She is afraid that Kenyatta will win the costume contest.

(G) She is unable to design her own costume for the contest.

(H) She is afraid to tell Kenyatta that she already has a costume.

(I) She fears that she will be embarrassed by wearing the costume.

3. What is the truth that Janelle tells Kenyatta?

(A) Janelle would rather stay at home than go to the festival.

(B) Janelle does not want to wear a costume like Kenyatta's.

(C) Janelle cannot think of anything to wear to the festival.

(D) Janelle feels bad that Kenyatta's costume always wins the contest.

4. Why does Janelle begin to draw at the end of the story?

(F) She has an idea for her own costume.

(G) She knows how to improve Kenyatta's costume.

(H) She is making a poster for the costume contest.

(I) She is designing a costume for Kenyatta.

Focus Skill: Make Inferences   146   TOTAL SCORE: _____ /4

Literary Patterns and Symbols

▶ **Read each passage. Then choose the best answer for each question.**

Owl and Hare

One beautiful autumn day, Hare was playing in a field and enjoying the brilliant sunshine. As he romped in the fallen leaves, he spotted Owl high up in a tree. He called out to Owl and asked him what he was doing on such a fine day.

"I am building my winter nest," Owl replied. "Today is warm and sunny, but winter will come very soon, so I have gathered grass and leaves to line my nest. My nest will be complete before everything becomes covered by snow."

"Owl, you should stop your efforts and enjoy the sun like me!" said Hare, but Owl continued working. That night, the cold wind blew and a thick layer of snow fell. While Hare shivered in his burrow, Owl appreciated his warm winter nest.

Beaver and Songbird

Every year when winter began turning to spring, Beaver worked day and night on his home. The melting snow made the river very powerful, and Beaver's home could be washed away if the walls were not thick and strong. From her warm nest, Songbird saw Beaver dragging branches across the snow.

"Beaver!" she called out, "It is too cold for working today. You should stay warm in your home like me and work on your nest tomorrow!" Beaver shook his head and worked on his home all through the cold, dark night.

The next day, the sun was bright and hot, and the snow melted quickly. The river rose, and the rapids splashed and foamed around Beaver's home, where he stayed safe inside.

1. How are the characters Hare and Songbird similar?
   Ⓐ Both tell other characters to put off their work.
   Ⓑ Both decide to work harder in the future.
   Ⓒ Both want to build stronger homes.
   Ⓓ Both try to trick another character in the story.

© Harcourt • Grade 5

2. What plot events repeat in both stories?

(F) Both begin with one character asking a difficult question.

(G) Both end with a character earning a reward.

(H) Both include animal characters preparing for a change of season.

(I) Both have characters that change during the story.

3. What ideas do Owl and Beaver represent?

(A) give helpful advice to others

(B) work and plan for the future

(C) learn to enjoy the present moment

(D) ignore the advice of others

4. What do the two stories have in common?

(F) Both tell about weather.

(G) Both have trickster characters.

(H) Both are amusing stories.

(I) Both teach the same lesson.

© Harcourt • Grade 5

Name _____

Robust Vocabulary

▶ **Choose the best word to complete each sentence.**

1. When Petra could not find her shoes in her closet, she was _____.
   - (A) proposed
   - (B) parched
   - (C) tempted
   - (D) baffled

2. Instead of doing her homework, Lucinda was _____ to play with her brother.
   - (F) tempted
   - (G) proposed
   - (H) baffled
   - (I) sustained

3. Michelle believed that trust was the _____ of a strong friendship.
   - (A) instinct
   - (B) essence
   - (C) indication
   - (D) elastic

4. Caesar's repeated yawns were an _____ that he had gotten little sleep last night.
   - (F) endeavor
   - (G) instinct
   - (H) essence
   - (I) indication

5. Because he had studied the artist's work, Mr. Parker had good _____ about the painting.
   - (A) indications
   - (B) escapades
   - (C) insights
   - (D) residents

Robust Vocabulary

149

6. The students used their extra time to begin their homework
as the teacher had _____.

   (F) proposed

   (G) tempted

   (H) recounted

   (I) conducted

7. Immediately after it is born, a kitten's first _____ is to begin feeding.

   (A) reputation

   (B) indication

   (C) instinct

   (D) essence

Name _____

Grammar: Subjective- and Objective-Case Pronouns

▶ **Choose the best answer for each question.**

1. Which is the subject pronoun in this sentence?

   She and Miguel returned the books to him.

   Ⓐ She
   Ⓑ Miguel
   Ⓒ books
   Ⓓ him

2. Which subject pronoun correctly completes this sentence?

   **After _____ took our coats to the closet, Selena hung
   them on hangers.**

   Ⓕ us
   Ⓖ he
   Ⓗ they
   Ⓘ we

3. Which is the object pronoun in this sentence?

   He gave us a surprise math test, on which we did well.

   Ⓐ He
   Ⓑ us
   Ⓒ math
   Ⓓ we

4. Which object pronoun correctly completes this sentence?

   **Daniel borrowed my pencil, and a few minutes later,
   he gave it back to _____.**

   Ⓕ we
   Ⓖ they
   Ⓗ me
   Ⓘ I

**Grammar: Subjective- and Objective-
Case Pronouns**

151

TOTAL SCORE: _____ /4

© Harcourt • Grade 5

Name _____

Oral Reading Fluency

Carlo enjoyed helping his father in the kitchen, and tonight they were planning to make a special meal. They had invited their new neighbors over for dinner, and Carlo and his father wanted to offer them a warm welcome to the neighborhood.

Carlo's father purchased food at the market and returned with three large paper bags, each filled to the brim. One bag was filled with a variety of vegetables for creating a sauce and a salad, another had a loaf of freshly baked Italian bread, and a third held several packages of chicken.

"Tonight, I will show you how to make a spectacular meal," said Carlo's father, delving into the bags. First, he demonstrated to Carlo how to combine vegetables and spices to make a thick sauce. While the sauce was simmering on the stove, Carlo's father prepared the chicken.

His father showed him how to sprinkle the chicken with cheese and breadcrumbs before he cooked the chicken in a pan until it was golden brown. When the chicken was done, Carlo helped his father make a large salad.

They finished making dinner just in time, and when their neighbors walked through the door, they could smell dinner cooking. The meal was delicious, and after dinner, the neighbors thanked Carlo and his father for giving them such a special gift.

© Harcourt • Grade 5

Selection Comprehension

▶ **Choose the best answer for each question.**

1. Which sentence BEST tells what the story is about?

   (A) Eva does not know what to write about for her teacher.

   (B) Eva waits for something to happen so she can write about it.

   (C) After Mr. Sims tells her to, Eva writes all the details she can recall.

   (D) When Eva follows advice, interesting events happen to write about.

2. Which word BEST describes the people in Eva's neighborhood?

   (F) gruff

   (G) humble

   (H) talented

   (I) threatening

3. Each person that Eva meets gives her advice based on his or her

   (A) hopes and fears.

   (B) interests or career.

   (C) school background.

   (D) publishing experience.

4. How do you know "Nothing Ever Happens on 90th Street" is realistic fiction?

   (F) It has acts that are divided into scenes.

   (G) It is the true story of a real person's life.

   (H) It takes place at a real time and place in the future.

   (I) It has characters with feelings that real people have.

5. How does Eva make something happen?

   (A) She stops the pizza delivery man.

   (B) She tosses a red ball into the street.

   (C) She throws pieces of Danish to the pigeons.

   (D) She spills coffee into Mr. Morley's mousse.

**Selection Comprehension
"Nothing Ever Happens on
90th Street"**

6. How are all of Eva's neighbors ALIKE?

Ⓕ All give writing ideas.

Ⓖ All have the same job.

Ⓗ All have a spoiled cat.

Ⓘ All are excellent cooks.

7. What is the result when Eva thinks of three great ideas?

Ⓐ More people move onto 90th Street.

Ⓑ Good things happen to her neighbors.

Ⓒ The Seafood Emporium has less business.

Ⓓ Mrs. de Marco lets her teach others to write.

8. What is Eva MOST LIKELY to do when she rewrites the story?

Ⓕ add some more "What ifs"

Ⓖ make more words rhyme

Ⓗ change to new characters

Ⓘ remove some of the details

Written Response

9. Which writing advice do you think helped Eva the MOST? Use details from "Nothing Ever Happens on 90th Street" to help you explain why you feel that advice was the most helpful.

_____

_____

_____

_____

_____

Selection Comprehension
"Nothing Ever Happens on
90th Street"

154

TOTAL SCORE: _____ /8 + _____ /2

© Harcourt • Grade 5

Focus Skill: Make Inferences

▶ Read the passage. Then choose the best answer for each question.

Samantha and the Chipmunks

As Samantha rode the bus home one day, she stared out the window at the world rushing past her. The trees, fields, and scattered houses all blurred together until the bus stopped, and then the world came into focus again. At one stop, she noticed an old oak tree near the road with a funny large bump on one side that was round, like a bowl. As she stared, four tiny baby chipmunks poked their heads out of the bump in the tree.

Samantha thought about the chipmunks for the rest of her ride home, wondering what it was like to live in a bump on the side of a tree. She searched her bag for blank paper and a pencil, but she had none. She frowned and stared back out the window.

Once she got off the bus, Samantha sprinted to her house, charged through the front door, yelled hello to her father, and bounded up the stairs to her bedroom. With great haste, she pulled a notebook and some pencils out of her desk.

Samantha wrote until her hand was cramped and her father called her for dinner. As she headed downstairs, she carried her notebook with her.

"Well, Samantha, what is the title of your latest story?" her father asked. Samantha opened the notebook and began to read.

"'Chipmunk Tales,' by Samantha Maloney. Chapter One: The Day We Discovered Our New Home."

1. The text says that the "trees, fields, and scattered houses all blurred together." What can you infer from this information?
   (A) The bus is moving quickly.
   (B) Samantha needs new glasses.
   (C) Rain is pouring outside.
   (D) Samantha has tears in her eyes.

Focus Skill: Make Inferences

2. Why does Samantha frown and stare out the bus window?

(F) She is upset that she must ride the bus home from school.

(G) She is worried about the amount of homework she must do.

(H) She is sad that she saw the chipmunks for only a short time.

(I) She is disappointed that she cannot find paper and a pencil.

3. The text says that Samantha "sprinted to her house" and "bounded up the stairs to her bedroom." What can you infer from this information?

(A) Samantha is trying to avoid talking to her father.

(B) Samantha is feeling a strong excitement to start writing.

(C) Samantha wants to finish her homework quickly.

(D) Samantha is tired and wants to go to bed early.

4. Which detail suggests that Samantha has written many stories?

(F) Samantha keeps a notebook and pencils for her stories.

(G) Samantha works on her story until her hand cramps.

(H) Samantha's father asks for the title of her latest story.

(I) Samantha's father enjoys hearing about her stories.

Focus Skill: Make Inferences

156

TOTAL SCORE: _____ /4

© Harcourt • Grade 5

Vocabulary Strategies: Synonyms and Antonyms

▶ **Choose the best answer for each question.**

1. Read this sentence.

   > The clouds overhead were reflected in the smooth surface of the lake.

   Which word is an antonym for the word *overhead*?
   - (A) behind
   - (B) under
   - (C) beside
   - (D) below

2. Read this sentence.

   > Ray saw what was happening, but it took Rachel a moment longer to realize that they had won the competition.

   Which word is a synonym for the word *realize*?
   - (F) forget
   - (G) understand
   - (H) suggest
   - (I) explain

3. Read this sentence.

   > Hannah felt exhausted after her hike up the trail, so she went to bed early.

   Which word is a synonym for the word *exhausted*?
   - (A) tired
   - (B) hungry
   - (C) lost
   - (D) bored

Vocabulary Strategies: Synonyms and Antonyms

157

© Harcourt • Grade 5

4. Read these sentences.

> Jacob was cautious while playing the game.
> Jaime was also paying close attention.

Which word is an antonym for the word *cautious*?

(F) careless

(G) quiet

(H) watchful

(I) carefree

5. Read this sentence.

> Kate felt drowsy while watching the movie, but Stephen
> was alert.

Which word is a synonym for the word *drowsy*?

(A) afraid

(B) sleepy

(C) lazy

(D) curious

6. Read this sentence.

> Irina had created a hulking pile of clothes on her floor,
> completely blocking the doorway.

Which word is an antonym for the word *hulking*?

(F) light

(G) dirty

(H) small

(I) colorful

**Vocabulary Strategies: Synonyms and
Antonyms**

TOTAL SCORE: _____ /6

© Harcourt • Grade 5

Name _____

Robust Vocabulary

▶ **Choose the best word to complete each sentence.**

1. Maya warned her friend that the broken chair was a _____ place to sit.
   - (A) hiatus
   - (B) parched
   - (C) baffled
   - (D) precarious

2. Antonio felt a thrill as he and his family _____ on their trip to the beach.
   - (F) proposed
   - (G) baffled
   - (H) embarked
   - (I) thronged

3. Sandra was a true _____ because she ate only the finest foods.
   - (A) gourmet
   - (B) resident
   - (C) hiatus
   - (D) outcast

4. Thomas's mother worked six days a week, so she was ready for a brief _____.
   - (F) throng
   - (G) hiatus
   - (H) instinct
   - (I) endeavor

Robust Vocabulary

© Harcourt • Grade 5

5. Niko enjoyed basketball so much that it was _____ to think of him playing any other sport.
   - (A) uninhabitable
   - (B) unimaginable
   - (C) precarious
   - (D) extravagant

6. Caitlin used what seemed like a ton of glitter and bright markers to make the _____ decorations for her party.
   - (F) rigid
   - (G) precarious
   - (H) monotonous
   - (I) extravagant

7. On a hot, sunny, summer day, a huge _____ of people always gathers at the beach.
   - (A) specimen
   - (B) essence
   - (C) throng
   - (D) hiatus

TOTAL SCORE: _____ /7

© Harcourt • Grade 5

Grammar: Possessive- and Reflexive-Case Pronouns

▶ **Choose the best answer for each question.**

1. Which possessive pronoun correctly completes this sentence?

   After he parked the truck, he reached for _____ toolbox on the passenger seat.

   (A) he
   (B) him
   (C) his
   (D) its

2. Which reflexive pronoun correctly completes this sentence?

   The teacher said to the class members, "You should ask _____ these questions to prepare for the test."

   (F) yourselves
   (G) yourself
   (H) itself
   (I) themselves

3. Which reflexive pronoun correctly completes this sentence?

   After finishing his project, Theo was proud that he had done all of it _____.

   (A) him
   (B) he
   (C) himself
   (D) hisself

4. Which possessive pronoun correctly completes this sentence?

   The students handed _____ papers to the substitute.

   (F) its
   (G) they
   (H) there
   (I) their

Oral Reading Fluency

Polar bears are large, white bears that live in northern areas where the climate is cold throughout the year. Polar bears look like other bears. However, polar bears are bigger than most other bears. In fact, they are among the largest meat-eating animals that walk on land. Adult polar bears can grow from six to ten feet tall and weigh more than one thousand pounds.

Polar bears are also unlike most other bears because polar bears are used to living in very cold conditions. To help them survive the cold climate, polar bears have a unique kind of fur. Their special fur keeps the water away from their skin and keeps them warm. Polar bears also have a layer of fat that insulates them from the freezing temperatures throughout the Arctic.

Polar bears live near the ocean, and despite the freezing weather, they still spend much of their time on the ice and in the water, hunting for seals to eat. Their white fur helps camouflage them when they hunt. Their sharp, strong claws help polar bears not only hunt but also maneuver in their icy world.

Because they have adapted to their frigid habitat, polar bears are sometimes called ice bears or sea bears.

© Harcourt • Grade 5

Selection Comprehension

▶ **Choose the best answer for each question.**

1. How do you know that "Project Mulberry" is realistic fiction?
   - (A) The story plot teaches a moral about life.
   - (B) The information is dependent upon photographs.
   - (C) The author's personal thoughts and feelings are expressed.
   - (D) The characters face problems that might happen in real life.

2. How does Julia react to Patrick's problem?
   - (F) She tries to make him hold a silkworm.
   - (G) She understands and respects his feelings.
   - (H) She talks to him about her fear of spiders.
   - (I) She hopes to talk him out of being afraid.

3. Why are Patrick and Julia unable to open the egg carton lids?
   - (A) Kenny has used glue to stick them together.
   - (B) The cartons cannot be lifted out of the aquarium.
   - (C) The egg cartons are too small for the caterpillars.
   - (D) Caterpillars have woven silk to the tops and bottoms.

4. Why does the author compare the early stage of the cocoon to a cloud?
   - (F) to prove it has a white color
   - (G) to show that it is very delicate
   - (H) to point out that it cannot be touched
   - (I) to explain that it is made of water vapor

5. What is the MAIN idea of "Project Mulberry"?
   - (A) A photographer can find a way to film anything.
   - (B) Good friends can create a prize-winning project.
   - (C) Watching silkworms make cocoons can be fascinating.
   - (D) Drawing the life cycle of a caterpillar is a good project.

6. Which action shows that Julia does NOT share Patrick's problem?

(F) She saves two egg cartons for the caterpillars.

(G) She quickly tapes up the hole in the egg carton.

(H) She uses nail scissors to poke a hole in the carton.

(I) She handles a caterpillar that comes out of the carton.

7. How does Patrick feel when Julia cuts the larger hole in the egg carton?

(A) frightened

(B) relaxed

(C) amused

(D) furious

8. How do you know that Patrick is MOST LIKELY a good student?

(F) He has learned everything he can about silkworms.

(G) He figures out how to film a caterpillar in a bottle.

(H) He knows how to film the silkworms when they make cocoons.

(I) He invites his family over to watch the caterpillar in the bottle.

READ THINK EXPLAIN

Written Response

9. Why would Julia be a good friend to have? Use examples and details from "Project Mulberry" to explain your answer.

_____

_____

_____

_____

_____

Focus Skill: Main Idea and Details

▶ **Read each paragraph. Then choose the best answer for each question.**

Love Those Lakes

During each season, there is a different reason to visit a lake. In an area with frigid winters, lakes usually freeze for part of the winter. Once they freeze thick enough to guarantee safety, they are fantastic for ice-skating, boot-sliding, or even ice fishing. After the ice thaws in spring, a lake is an ideal place to catch tadpoles, or baby frogs. In the warm summer months, lakes are good places to go swimming to cool off. It is too cold to swim in most lakes in autumn, but lakes are still good spots for boating or fishing.

1. Which sentence states the main idea of the paragraph?
   Ⓐ "During each season, there is a different reason to visit a lake."
   Ⓑ "In an area with frigid winters, lakes usually freeze for part of the winter."
   Ⓒ "After the ice thaws in spring, a lake is an ideal place to catch tadpoles, or baby frogs."
   Ⓓ "It is too cold to swim in most lakes in autumn, but lakes are still good spots for boating or fishing."

2. How does each detail support the main idea of the paragraph?
   Ⓕ Each detail describes a different lake.
   Ⓖ Each detail gives a different reason to visit a lake in each season.
   Ⓗ Each detail shows how lakes are easy to find on a map.
   Ⓘ Each detail explains what to do at a lake in winter.

© Harcourt • Grade 5

How to Care for Kittens

A mother cat has instincts about how to raise her kittens, but there are still a few ways that you can help her care for her young. First, you can help keep her kittens warm and comfortable by creating a bed lined with blankets or towels. Second, you can help the mother cat feel safe by keeping other animals away from her kittens. Finally, you can help teach the kittens how to behave around people. If you play with the kittens each day once they can walk, they will learn to trust and enjoy people, making them ideal family pets.

3. Which sentence states the main idea of the paragraph?

   (A) "First, you can help keep her kittens warm and comfortable by creating a bed lined with blankets or towels."

   (B) "Second, you can help the mother cat feel safe by keeping other animals away from her kittens."

   (C) "A mother cat has instincts about how to raise her kittens, but there are still a few ways that you can help her care for her young."

   (D) "If you play with the kittens each day once they can walk, they will learn to trust and enjoy people, making them ideal family pets."

4. How does each detail support the main idea of the paragraph?

   (F) Each detail tells what kittens need to stay warm and comfortable.

   (G) Each detail explains how a mother cat cares for her kittens.

   (H) Each detail describes how to help kittens become great family pets.

   (I) Each detail shows a way to help a mother cat care for her kittens.

Main Idea and Details

TOTAL SCORE: _____ /4

© Harcourt • Grade 5

Name _____

Point of View

▶ **Read each passage. Then choose the best answer for each question.**

I carefully inspected the branches overhead, trying to find the perfect specimen. Its color had to be mostly red and rosy, with just a hint of green. It needed to feel firm to the touch, not soft or mushy. Its skin could have no flaws—no bruises or cuts. It also had to be large enough to fill the palm of my hand, but not too big to be eaten for a snack. After looking over more than a dozen specimens, something caught my attention from deep inside the leafy green branches. With a nimble gesture, I reached in and plucked the perfect apple.

1. What is the point of view of this story?
   (A) first-person
   (B) second-person
   (C) third-person limited
   (D) third-person omniscient

2. How do you know the point of view of this story?
   (F) The narrator describes an object in the story.
   (G) The narrator changes in different parts of the story.
   (H) The narrator is not a character in the story.
   (I) The narrator uses the pronoun *I* in the story.

© Harcourt • Grade 5

As Mr. Leppanen's class walked through the orange grove, Hiroko studied each of the trees they passed. *Last year Shane found the perfect orange,* she thought, *and this year I am determined to do the same.* She was so absorbed in her thoughts that she barely noticed her friend behind her.

Shane walked a few steps behind Hiroko, but he was not studying the trees. He knew that the best orange tree in the grove was in the third row on the right side, next to the white fence. He smiled to himself and thought, *Hiroko will be so surprised when I let her find the perfect orange.*

3. What is the point of view of this story?
   (A) first-person
   (B) second-person
   (C) third-person limited
   (D) third-person omniscient

4. How do you know the point of view of this story?
   (F) The narrator changes in different parts of the story.
   (G) The narrator knows what all the characters are thinking.
   (H) The narrator uses the pronouns *she* and *he*.
   (I) The narrator uses the pronoun *I*.

© Harcourt • Grade 5

Vocabulary Strategies: Synonyms and Antonyms

▶ **Choose the best answer for each question.**

1. Read this sentence.

    She was feeling bewildered.

    Which word is a synonym for *bewildered*?
    - Ⓐ puzzled
    - Ⓑ lonely
    - Ⓒ ashamed
    - Ⓓ anxious

2. Read this sentence.

    He made an earnest attempt.

    Which word is a synonym for *earnest*?
    - Ⓕ yearning
    - Ⓖ sincere
    - Ⓗ patient
    - Ⓘ grim

3. Read this sentence.

    The stagnant air smelled horrible.

    Which word is an antonym for *stagnant*?
    - Ⓐ clear
    - Ⓑ dry
    - Ⓒ flowing
    - Ⓓ dirty

4. Read this phrase.

    the delicate leaf

    Which word is a synonym for *delicate*?
    - Ⓕ fragile
    - Ⓖ smooth
    - Ⓗ rough
    - Ⓘ sturdy

5. Read this phrase.

her serious mood

Which word is an antonym for *serious*?

(A) businesslike

(B) intelligent

(C) cheerful

(D) determined

6. Read this phrase.

the plump geese

Which word is an antonym for *plump*?

(F) fast

(G) rough

(H) slender

(I) silent

Robust Vocabulary

▶ **Choose the best word to complete each sentence.**

1. Because it might disturb some students, the teacher _____ the idea
   to play music during the test.
   - (A) swayed
   - (B) embarked
   - (C) vetoed
   - (D) tempted

2. The campers went into their tents to escape the sudden _____ of
   mosquitoes.
   - (F) hiatus
   - (G) invasion
   - (H) instinct
   - (I) phobia

3. Alexandra's grandmother kept her jewelry in a special box with many
   small _____.
   - (A) invasions
   - (B) residents
   - (C) compartments
   - (D) throngs

4. A newborn baby's hair is usually soft and _____.
   - (F) rigid
   - (G) swaying
   - (H) precarious
   - (I) wispy

© Harcourt • Grade 5

5. My brother avoided closets because he had a strong
_____ about small spaces.

   (A) phobia

   (B) instinct

   (C) hiatus

   (D) invasion

6. The branches of the trees _____ in the gentle breeze.

   (F) proposed

   (G) embarked

   (H) vetoed

   (I) swayed

TOTAL SCORE: _____ /6

© Harcourt • Grade 5

Grammar: Adjectives and Articles

▶ **Choose the best answer for each question.**

1. Which word is an adjective in this sentence?

   Paulo wore a colorful sweater to school.

   (A) wore

   (B) colorful

   (C) sweater

   (D) a

2. Which article correctly completes this sentence?

   Kathryn wrote about _____ first cat she ever owned.

   (F) a

   (G) an

   (H) the

   (I) some

3. Which adjective or adjective phrase correctly completes this sentence?

   Tyrell was _____ about the project than Devin was.

   (A) more excited

   (B) exciteder

   (C) most excited

   (D) excitedest

4. Which adjective or adjective phrase correctly completes this sentence?

   Miss Politis was the _____ science teacher in the school.

   (F) bestest

   (G) most better

   (H) best

   (I) most best

TOTAL SCORE: _____ /4

© Harcourt • Grade 5

Oral Reading Fluency

One day in art class, Salvador learned about a famous artist from France. His teacher displayed some of this artist's paintings, which showed vivid scenes from cities and towns. The artist used bright colors such as blue and yellow, and he applied thick layers of paint.

After they admired the paintings, the class had the opportunity to create their own masterpieces. Salvador decided to paint his grandmother's home in Mexico, which he had always hoped to visit. Because he liked the bright colors that the artist had used, he chose to use red, yellow, and blue paints to make his grandmother's home appear as vivid as the scenes he had seen in the paintings.

Salvador combined red and yellow paint to create a deep shade of orange, which he used to paint the walls of the house. Then he used a darker red to paint the roof. When the house was complete, Salvador began painting the yard.

He mixed the blue and yellow to make the bright green of the plants in his grandmother's yard, and then he made red and yellow dots for flowers among the green. Finally, he put a bright yellow sun in the sky, and he signed his name at the bottom.

Salvador was very pleased with his masterpiece and decided to make the painting a special gift to his grandmother.

_____ /WCPM

Selection Comprehension

▶ **Choose the best answer for each question.**

1. How do you know that "Inventing the Future" is a biography?
   (A) The characters' actions and feelings are shown through dialogue.
   (B) The reader is challenged to find an answer to a problem.
   (C) Information is given about why a person is important.
   (D) Information is divided into sections with headings.

2. Which detail BEST shows that Edison liked inventing, even as a child?
   (F) He often used to daydream during his classes.
   (G) He used a picture as a guide to build his own telegraph set.
   (H) He practiced sending coded messages to and from a friend.
   (I) He began selling newspapers on the Grand Trunk Railway.

3. It is MOST LIKELY that Edison made his inventions in order to
   (A) satisfy his curiosity.
   (B) become wealthy.
   (C) make friends.
   (D) gain fame.

4. The author included photographs of Edison and his family MAINLY to
   (F) help readers understand more about the inventor.
   (G) illustrate the clothing people wore in the 1800s.
   (H) show what an inventor usually looks like.
   (I) contrast life of long ago with life today.

5. As a boy, Edison liked to perform the experiments he read about in his textbook MAINLY because he wanted to
   (A) invent electrical instruments.
   (B) see if the facts were accurate.
   (C) mix chemicals and acids.
   (D) learn how things worked.

6. The author tells that Edison bought 1,000 newspapers describing the battle at Shiloh MAINLY to show that Edison

   F was quick to see opportunities.

   G lived during exciting times.

   H could make money easily.

   I cared about other people.

7. What is the MOST LIKELY reason Edison wanted to learn to be a telegraph operator?

   A His work on trains had become boring.

   B He planned to invent a similar machine.

   C He knew he could get a job almost anywhere.

   D He hoped to teach others to translate messages.

8. Why did Edison often lose his job as a "tramp telegrapher"?

   F He took too many catnaps during the day.

   G He liked experimenting more than working.

   H He wrote too slowly to record the messages.

   I He was unable to keep the equipment working.

Written Response

9. **COMPARING TEXTS** What qualities did Edison have that helped him succeed? Use details from "Inventing the Future" and "Letter from Thomas Edison to Henry Ford" to support your answer.

_____

_____

_____

_____

_____

_____

**Selection Comprehension
"Inventing the Future"**

176

TOTAL SCORE: _____ /8 + _____ /2

Focus Skill: Main Idea and Details

▶ **Read each paragraph. Then choose the best answer for each
question.**

Juan Ponce de León

For centuries, people have told the story of how the explorer Ponce de
León discovering what is now Florida by accident. He had heard that the
legendary Fountain of Youth was located on a nearby island. Anyone who
drank from this fountain would never grow old. He sailed out to sea to
begin his quest for this famous fountain. When his ship reached land, he
was amazed by all of the beautiful flowers he saw. He decided to name the
area *Florida*, which means "flowery." Although he found a beautiful land,
he did not find the fountain he was seeking. He returned to Florida seven
years later to try to find the fountain again, but he was unsuccessful.

1. What is the main idea of this paragraph?
   - (A) Ponce de León began the legend of the Fountain of Youth.
   - (B) Ponce de León set sail for Florida and the islands nearby to find
flowers.
   - (C) Ponce de León was unable to find the Fountain of Youth.
   - (D) Ponce de León discovered Florida while seeking the Fountain of
Youth.

2. Which detail from the paragraph best supports the main idea?
   - (F) The Fountain of Youth had special powers.
   - (G) The name *Florida* means "flowery."
   - (H) Ponce de León found Florida by accident.
   - (I) Ponce de León heard about the Fountain of Youth.

© Harcourt • Grade 5

Giraffe Facts

Giraffes are excellent survivors. They live in areas of Africa that receive very little rain, and although many animals must drink water every day, giraffes can go without water for long periods of time. When they cannot find water to drink, they drink dew, which is the tiny drops of water that coat grass and other plants early in the morning. Giraffes can also get water from the leaves that they eat. Their very long necks enable them to eat the leaves from the upper branches of trees. Giraffes also have very good eyesight, and they can see for long distances. This helps them watch out for dangerous animals.

3. What is this paragraph mostly about?

(A) how giraffes eat leaves from tall trees

(B) how giraffes endure a difficult environment

(C) how giraffes can live on very little water

(D) how giraffes watch out for other animals

4. Which sentence is the main idea sentence of this paragraph?

(F) "Giraffes are excellent survivors."

(G) "Giraffes can also get water from the leaves that they eat."

(H) "Their very long necks enable them to eat the leaves from the upper branches of trees."

(I) "Giraffes also have very good eyesight, and they can see for long distances."

TOTAL SCORE: _____ /4

© Harcourt • Grade 5

Point of View

▶ **Read the passage. Then choose the best answer for each question.**

Dr. Sally Ride

Sally Ride is a famous astronaut and a true American hero. In 1983, she was part of the crew of the space shuttle *Challenger*. Along with the rest of the crew, she experienced the launch into space and many orbits around Earth. She was the first American woman to perform the incredible feat of traveling in space.

Becoming an astronaut was not a childhood dream for Sally Ride. Instead, she wanted to be a tennis player. In college, she became interested in studying science. She was especially interested in the type of science that has to do with space. After she finished college, she decided to apply for a job as an astronaut.

On her first *Challenger* mission, Sally Ride spent six days in space. She completed several experiments and fulfilled other important tasks on the shuttle. She also helped release satellites by using the shuttle's "arm," which reached out into space. When she returned, she said she had just had "the most fun I'll ever have in my life."

Sally Ride has done great things both in space and on Earth. In 1989, she decided to share with others what she had learned. She became a teacher at a college, and she also worked on programs that made science fun for children.

1. What is the point of view of this passage?
   (A) first-person
   (B) second-person
   (C) third-person limited
   (D) third-person omniscient

2. How do you know the point of view of this passage?
   (F) The narrator appears as a character in the passage.
   (G) The narrator knows many characters well in the passage.
   (H) The narrator uses the pronoun *I* in the passage.
   (I) The narrator knows one character well in the passage.

© Harcourt • Grade 5

3. What is the author's perspective on Sally Ride?

  (A) The author admires Sally Ride for her achievements.

  (B) The author wishes to work with Sally Ride in the future.

  (C) The author finds Sally Ride's experiences amusing.

  (D) The author wants to learn more about Sally Ride.

4. Which line from the passage shows the author's perspective?

  (F) "She was the first American woman to perform the incredible feat of traveling in space."

  (G) "On her first *Challenger* mission, Sally Ride spent six days in space."

  (H) "Sally Ride has done great things both in space and on Earth."

  (I) "In 1989, she decided to share with others what she had learned."

© Harcourt • Grade 5

Name _____

Robust Vocabulary

▶ **Choose the best word to complete each sentence.**

1. On the first warm spring day, Carmen felt an _____ urge to go outside.

   Ⓐ irrepressible
   Ⓑ extravagant
   Ⓒ intricate
   Ⓓ industrious

2. To sail all the way around the world is a difficult _____.

   Ⓕ industry
   Ⓖ phobia
   Ⓗ feat
   Ⓘ device

3. When he was nervous, Blane had a _____ to laugh.

   Ⓐ device
   Ⓑ tendency
   Ⓒ feat
   Ⓓ throng

4. The cotton gin was a _____ that made it easier and faster to clean cotton.

   Ⓕ feat
   Ⓖ device
   Ⓗ specimen
   Ⓘ compartment

Robust Vocabulary

© Harcourt • Grade 5

Name _____

5. Because he loves music, Abdul hopes to work in the music
   _____.

   (A) hiatus
   (B) compartment
   (C) industry
   (D) device

6. The job of President is one of the most _____ positions in
   our government.

   (F) unfathomable
   (G) monotonous
   (H) irrepressible
   (I) prestigious

Robust Vocabulary   182   TOTAL SCORE: _____ /6

Name _____

Grammar: Main and Helping Verbs

▶ **Choose the best answer for each question.**

1. Read this sentence.

   He will write his name on the next page.

   Which word is the main verb in the sentence?

   (A) will

   (B) write

   (C) on

   (D) next

2. Which verb correctly completes this sentence?

   She will _____ all of her homework.

   (F) finished

   (G) finishing

   (H) finish

   (I) finishes

3. Read this sentence.

   My mother will drive me to school in the morning.

   Which word is the helping verb in the sentence?

   (A) will

   (B) drive

   (C) in

   (D) the

4. Which verb correctly completes this sentence?

   He will _____ the book to the library.

   (F) returned

   (G) returning

   (H) returns

   (I) return

Grammar: Main and Helping Verbs   183   TOTAL SCORE: _____ /4

Oral Reading Fluency

The first woman to fly over the North Pole was an American named Louise Boyd. She was born in California in 1887. Louise grew up with a love of travel, and when she was an adult, she began exploring the world.

Louise was especially interested in exploring the Arctic. One of the coldest places in the world, this area around the North Pole is covered with ice and snow throughout the year.

Louise admired other explorers who had visited this cold but interesting place, and on one of her first trips to the Arctic, Louise helped search for another explorer who was missing. Although she did not find him, she received an award for her efforts. After that, she made several trips to study the Arctic Ocean and its coastal areas.

Louise made a number of important discoveries on her trips. For example, near Greenland she found an island that was later named after her, and she located an underwater ridge hidden deep in the ocean.

At the age of 68, Louise set a new record when she became the first woman to fly in a plane over the North Pole. She wrote three books and many articles about her numerous amazing experiences in the Arctic.

© Harcourt • Grade 5

Name _____

Selection Comprehension

▶ **Choose the best answer for each question.**

1. What is the MAIN problem in "The Invention Convention"?
   Ⓐ The event is very crowded.
   Ⓑ The audience likes all the inventions.
   Ⓒ The Invention of the Year must be chosen.
   Ⓓ The "Choosy Box" will not release the nametags.

2. Why did the author write "The Invention Convention"?
   Ⓕ to contrast two similar inventions
   Ⓖ to explain what a convention is like
   Ⓗ to tell about some unusual inventions
   Ⓘ to persuade readers to become inventors

3. It is MOST LIKELY that the "Choosy Box" won last year's award because it was
   Ⓐ fun to use.
   Ⓑ easy to carry.
   Ⓒ simple to make.
   Ⓓ brightly colored.

4. Jeffrey suggests changing the "No Oops! Spoon" because he
   Ⓕ wants to impress Elijah.
   Ⓖ likes to improve inventions.
   Ⓗ wishes the invention were his.
   Ⓘ thinks the invention will not work.

5. To win the contest in "The Invention Convention," it is MOST important to
   Ⓐ be physically fit.
   Ⓑ be full of confidence.
   Ⓒ have a vivid imagination.
   Ⓓ have a good sense of humor.

6. The MOST LIKELY reason the names of the inventions have repeated letters or sounds is because

(F) the names will help buyers remember the product.

(G) the audience will think the idea is clever.

(H) the names will look good on a billboard.

(I) the inventions make unusual noises.

7. What is one problem with the "Rover Reminder"?

(A) It comes in only one color.

(B) It is available only for dogs.

(C) It can be found in few stores.

(D) It is difficult to hear the sounds.

8. Which detail would be MOST important to include in a summary of "The Invention Convention"?

(F) Hope is from Raleigh, North Carolina.

(G) Inventions can be unusual, but they must also be useful.

(H) Carmela just heard about the convention last week.

(I) There are so many people that it seems like an invasion of inventors.

READ THINK EXPLAIN **Written Response**

9. If you were judging the contest, which invention would you choose as the Invention of the Year? Explain why you would choose that invention as the winner. Use details from "The Invention Convention" to support your answer.

_____

_____

_____

_____

_____

Name _____

Robust Vocabulary

▶ **Choose the best word to complete each sentence.**

1. Wearing a warm jacket, gloves, and a hat in very cold weather
   is _____.
   (A) portable
   (B) boisterous
   (C) fickle
   (D) practical

2. Following the rules and respecting others are _____ behaviors in
   school.
   (F) measly
   (G) boisterous
   (H) appropriate
   (I) portable

3. After each meal, Dale _____ the dirty pots and pans until they
   gleam.
   (A) embarks
   (B) circulates
   (C) sways
   (D) scours

4. The science teacher explained how the heart helps blood _____
   throughout the body.
   (F) sway
   (G) protrude
   (H) circulate
   (I) embark

5. Because it runs on batteries, a _____ radio is perfect for camping.
   (A) boisterous
   (B) portable
   (C) fickle
   (D) measly

Robust Vocabulary

187

6. The movers worried that the huge couch would _____ from the back of their small truck.

   (F) protrude

   (G) veto

   (H) circulate

   (I) embark

7. The weather was sunny one minute and raining the next; the weather was _____ today.

   (A) boisterous

   (B) fickle

   (C) portable

   (D) measly

8. After paying a high price for a small amount of food, Mario told us the restaurant served _____ meals.

   (F) practical

   (G) portable

   (H) fickle

   (I) measly

9. When the players could not hear, the referee asked the _____ crowd to quiet down.

   (A) portable

   (B) boisterous

   (C) practical

   (D) measly

10. A good detective uses her powers of _____ to solve a mystery.

   (F) deduction

   (G) industry

   (H) circulation

   (I) invasion

© Harcourt • Grade 5

Selection Comprehension

▶ **Choose the best answer for each question.**

1. How do you know that "Interrupted Journey" is nonfiction?
   - (A) It has facts and details about a specific subject.
   - (B) It has realistic characters and events from the past.
   - (C) It tells the author's personal thoughts and feelings.
   - (D) It gives information about why a person is important.

2. What is the MAIN reason the author wrote "Interrupted Journey"?
   - (F) to tell a story about a marine animal in Florida
   - (G) to explain how people are helping certain animals
   - (H) to show why winter is dangerous for some animals
   - (I) to describe a special kind of animal hospital in Florida

3. With which statement would the author MOST LIKELY agree?
   - (A) Looking for turtles in winter is a difficult task.
   - (B) Cape Cod beaches are unpleasant in the winter.
   - (C) Children can find vanishing species more easily than adults.
   - (D) It is important to try to save animals that are in danger.

4. What do volunteers do LAST when they find a dying turtle on Ellis Landing Beach?
   - (F) call the sea-turtle rescue line
   - (G) protect the turtle with seaweed
   - (H) mark the turtle's location with a stick
   - (I) move the turtle above the high tide mark

5. Why is the turtle Max found sent to the New England Aquarium?
   - (A) They need turtles for a new exhibit there.
   - (B) The doctors there are good at treating turtles.
   - (C) It is the only place with a wading pool for turtles.
   - (D) It is the closest place to where the turtle was found.

6. Based on the article, what is the MAIN reason it is hard to tell if a turtle is alive?

(F) Its heartbeat can be very slow.

(G) Its slow movements are difficult to see.

(H) It is often covered by algae and seaweed.

(I) It usually has a very low body temperature.

7. The dangers a turtle might face in the Florida Keys are MOSTLY caused by

(A) other turtles.

(B) sharks.

(C) people.

(D) weather.

8. Which fact would be MOST important to include in a summary of "Interrupted Journey"?

(F) Wind makes Max's eyes sting as he patrols the beach.

(G) It is close to Thanksgiving when Max finds a turtle.

(H) All sea turtles are threatened or endangered.

(I) Pilgrims once walked on a Cape Cod beach.

Written Response

9. Why is Richie Moretti probably BOTH happy and worried when he releases Yellow-Blue at the end of the article? Use details from "Interrupted Journey" to help you explain.

_____

_____

_____

_____

Focus Skill: Author's Purpose and Perspective

▶ Read the passage. Then choose the best answer for each
question.

Old Dogs Are Good Dogs

You may have heard the saying, "You can't teach an old dog new
tricks." I cannot say whether this is true, but I know that an old dog *can*
make an excellent companion. If you are thinking of adopting a dog, there
are many good reasons to choose an older dog over a puppy.

One good reason is that older dogs are calmer than most puppies.
Puppies might chew on shoes or furniture when they are bored, and they
will not be content to stay inside for long periods of time, but older dogs
need more rest and are not always anxious for action. They need less
attention and are easier to take care of, which is helpful if you have a busy
life.

More importantly, the older the dog, the less chance it has of being
adopted. Most people want to adopt a puppy; therefore, older dogs at
shelters often remain homeless. By adopting an older dog, you are making
a difference in a dog's life.

Two years ago, I adopted an old dog named Sebastian, and he has
become my good friend. He likes to play and go for walks, but most of all
he likes to be with me. The next time you're thinking of adopting a dog,
consider an older dog. You'll be glad you did.

1. Why do you think the author mentions puppies in the second
   paragraph?
   (A) to show that older dogs are easier to care for than puppies
   (B) to show why more people choose to adopt puppies
   (C) to show how much fun owning a puppy can be
   (D) to show how to give a puppy excellent care

2. Why does the author describe Sebastian in the last paragraph?
   (F) to explain why the author thinks puppies require too much work
   (G) to explain why older dogs are usually easy to care for
   (H) to show that the author has experience with an older dog
   (I) to show that sometimes an older dog is the wrong choice

3. How does the author feel about adopting older dogs?

(A) Adopting an older dog is a great deal of work.

(B) People should adopt only older dogs.

(C) Adopting an older dog takes time and money.

(D) More people should adopt older dogs.

4. Which sentence reveals the author's perspective?

(F) "You may have heard the saying, 'You can't teach an old dog new tricks.'"

(G) "If you are thinking of adopting a dog, there are many good reasons to choose an older dog over a puppy."

(H) "Most people want to adopt a puppy; therefore, older dogs at shelters often remain homeless."

(I) "He likes to play and go for walks, but most of all he likes to be with me."

Name _____

Robust Vocabulary

▶ **Choose the best word to complete each sentence.**

1. Marta's cat was always sitting on the windowsill, _____ in the sun.
   - (A) analyzing
   - (B) basking
   - (C) swaying
   - (D) protruding

2. The coach said that it was _____ for the team to practice in order to improve.
   - (F) sleek
   - (G) vital
   - (H) prestigious
   - (I) fickle

3. The science class is _____ frogs to learn how they eat, sleep, and move.
   - (A) basking
   - (B) tempting
   - (C) analyzing
   - (D) circulating

4. Talib brushed his dog's fur until it looked shiny and _____.
   - (F) wispy
   - (G) sleek
   - (H) vital
   - (I) practical

Robust Vocabulary

© Harcourt • Grade 5

5. Becca had to look carefully to _____ the tiny spot of paint
   on the floor.

   Ⓐ sway

   Ⓑ deduce

   Ⓒ detect

   Ⓓ veto

6. Amir handled the fragile paper very carefully so that he would
   not _____ it.

   Ⓕ detect

   Ⓖ embark

   Ⓗ tempt

   Ⓘ damage

TOTAL SCORE: _____ /6

Name _____

Grammar: Action and Linking Verbs

▶ **Choose the best answer for each question.**

1. Which sentence has an action verb?
   (A) She yawned loudly.
   (B) He seems friendly.
   (C) I feel happy today.
   (D) She appeared confused.

2. Which sentence has a linking verb?
   (F) I dove into the heated water of the pool.
   (G) They paddled the boat downstream.
   (H) He is a math teacher at our school.
   (I) She dangled the rope in front of the dog.

3. Which verb correctly completes this sentence?

   The swimmers _____ fifth-graders at Palm Elementary.

   (A) be
   (B) are
   (C) was
   (D) is

4. Which verb correctly completes this sentence?

   She has _____ reading a story from the assignment list.

   (F) were
   (G) are
   (H) be
   (I) been

Grammar: Action and Linking Verbs 195 **TOTAL SCORE: _____ /4**

Oral Reading Fluency

"Today we are going to learn about igloos," said Mrs. Eady. "Igloos are houses that Artic peoples build out of snow, and you are going to construct your own igloo, here in our classroom!"

Mrs. Eady hung a picture of an igloo on the board, and the students saw that it was shaped like a large upside-down bowl. Instead of a door, there was a hole cut in one side, and covered by a small arch.

The students wondered how they were going to build a house out of snow, because it rarely snowed where they lived, even in the winter. Suddenly, Mrs. Eady began pulling empty plastic milk jugs out of the closet, and she explained that they were going to glue the milk jugs together to assemble the igloo.

The class began by placing a row of milk jugs in a circle, leaving a space for the opening. Then, Mrs. Eady showed them how to use the strong glue to attach the jugs together. They built a second row on top, and then a third row, each a little bit smaller than the row below. Before long, they had built a milk jug igloo that they could all fit inside, and they were extremely proud of their accomplishment.

© Harcourt • Grade 5

Selection Comprehension

▶ **Choose the best answer for each question.**

1. How do you know that "The Power of W.O.W.!" is a play?

    Ⓐ The information depends on photographs.

    Ⓑ It explains how people and places came to be.

    Ⓒ It contains information about a specific topic.

    Ⓓ The characters' actions and feelings are shown through dialogue.

2. What does the author MOST LIKELY assume about the reader?

    Ⓕ The reader is familiar with libraries.

    Ⓖ The reader knows how to use computers.

    Ⓗ The reader has volunteered at a bake sale.

    Ⓘ The reader has raised money at a car wash.

3. Why did the author write "The Power of W.O.W.!"?

    Ⓐ to tell about some students who were determined

    Ⓑ to describe what a bookmobile looks like inside

    Ⓒ to persuade students to do a community project

    Ⓓ to teach about different ways to raise money

4. Why do the students decide to take flyers to the businesses in town?

    Ⓕ They want Mr. Diaz to give them some orange cake.

    Ⓖ They want to collect money for cleaning supplies.

    Ⓗ They have read about ways to raise funds.

    Ⓘ They know the owners will donate money.

5. Which action BEST shows that Maria Kopanas believes in what Ileana is doing?

    Ⓐ She knows about P.O.W.W.O.W.

    Ⓑ She asks about the bookmobile.

    Ⓒ She interviews Erica and Jake.

    Ⓓ She thinks the news van needs a good wash.

6. Which action BEST shows that Mrs. Nguyen is a good librarian?

(F) She knows how to drive the bookmobile.

(G) She wants to help raise money for W.O.W.

(H) She knows which books each person would like.

(I) She allows Jake to use the computer in the bookmobile.

7. At the beginning of the play, what is the MOST LIKELY reason that no one has given money to W.O.W.?

(A) They want to go downtown to the library.

(B) They are unaware of the funding problem.

(C) They think that the bookmobile is unimportant.

(D) They have their own computers and books at home.

8. At the end of the play, which word BEST describes the people in the community?

(F) generous

(G) grateful

(H) astonished

(I) cautious

READ THINK EXPLAIN **Written Response**

9. Explain why the students were successful in saving the Words on Wheels program. Use details from "The Power of W.O.W.!" to help you explain.

_____

_____

_____

_____

_____

Name _____

Focus Skill: Author's Purpose and Perspective

▶ Read the passage. Then choose the best answer for each
question.

Sand Sculptures

Early one June morning, Alberto and his older sister Dominique
were eating breakfast when their father suddenly burst into the kitchen,
looking exhilarated. He was carrying the large cooler they used on family
outings, which had been stored in the garage.

"Hurry up and eat your breakfast! We're going to the beach!" he
announced. They cheered, because they had been anxious for a trip to the
beach for some time. Alberto was especially looking forward to playing
beach volleyball. They helped their father prepare sandwiches and pack
up the car. Soon they were on their way, looking forward to the sun, sand,
and surf.

At the beach, Dominique and Alberto immediately raced to the
water; but it was too cold for swimming, so Alberto decided it was time
for a game of volleyball. He searched through the bags, but finding that
the equipment was missing, he sat down on his towel, disappointed. He
had nothing to do; he had even forgotten his surfboard at home. Then,
Dominique called Alberto over to the water's edge.

"Alberto," she said, "there are other things to do at the beach. Watch
this!" Dominique showed Alberto how to sculpt sand with shells and
sticks. Alberto was excited, and soon he had created a spacecraft in the
sand. That day, Alberto learned that with a clever imagination, a person
can always have fun.

1. Why does the author have Dominique teach Alberto to make sand
   sculptures?
   Ⓐ to show how important it is to plan ahead
   Ⓑ to persuade older children to help younger children
   Ⓒ to show how a person can change their experience
   Ⓓ to entertain with a series of funny events

2. How does the author feel about being creative?

   (F) It is something that is learned from others.

   (G) It is something that develops over time.

   (H) It can change any person into an artist.

   (I) It can help a person enjoy any situation.

3. Which line from the story shows the author's perspective?

   (A) "They cheered because they had been anxious for a trip to the beach."

   (B) "Soon they were on their way, looking forward to the sun, sand, and surf."

   (C) "He searched through the bags, but finding that the equipment was missing, he sat down on his towel, disappointed."

   (D) "That day, Alberto learned that with a clever imagination, a person can always have fun."

4. Why did the author write this story?

   (F) to teach a lesson

   (G) to persuade

   (H) to inform

   (I) to give instructions

Draw Conclusions

▶ **Read the passage. Then choose the best answer for each question.**

Niran and the Ladder

Niran's mother decided to take advantage of the good weather to work on their house. Some of the wooden shingles on one side of the house were old and rotten; therefore, she wanted to replace them. Because Niran enjoyed working on projects with his mother, he offered to help.

Niran was surprised when his mother put on her gloves, walked up to the side of the house, took hold of a shingle, and ripped it off. After she explained that it was the easiest and most efficient way to remove the old wood, Niran put on his gloves and joined her. Soon they had cleared the entire wall as high as they could reach.

Next, Niran's mother had him rake the old wood away from the house as she securely set up two tall ladders. She climbed one of the ladders and continued removing the shingles.

Niran knew the second ladder was meant for him, but when he tried to put one foot on the bottom rung, his feet were glued in place. No matter how hard he tried, he could not convince himself to climb any higher.

His mother watched him for a moment and said, "Niran, I can easily finish this by myself, so why don't you just continue raking? That way, we can accomplish two tasks at the same time!" Niran smiled, thinking how much he enjoyed working with his mother.

1. Which detail explains why Niran cannot climb the ladder?
   (A) Niran feels that his feet have become stuck when he tries to climb.
   (B) Niran is surprised when his mother rips a shingle off of the house.
   (C) Niran must continue raking the old wood away from the house.
   (D) Niran's mother sinks the feet of both ladders into the ground.

© Harcourt • Grade 5

2. What conclusion can you draw about Niran and the ladder?

  (F) His sneaker stuck to the ladder when he stepped on it.

  (G) His ladder is not as strong as his mother's ladder.

  (H) He feels nervous about climbing the ladder.

  (I) He has climbed ladders many times in the past.

3. Which detail explains why Niran's mother asks him to continue raking?

  (A) She decides to work while the weather is good.

  (B) She and Niran clear the entire wall of the shingles.

  (C) She safely sets up two ladders on the ground.

  (D) She watches as Niran tries to climb the ladder.

4. What conclusion can you draw about Niran's mother?

  (F) She thinks that she can work much faster on her own.

  (G) She thinks that Niran enjoys raking the shingles.

  (H) She understands that Niran is tired of their project.

  (I) She understands that Niran fears climbing the ladder.

© Harcourt • Grade 5

Name _____

Robust Vocabulary

▶ **Choose the best word to complete each sentence.**

1. Young children must be taught to share toys, rather than _____ them.
   - (A) monopolize
   - (B) deflate
   - (C) analyze
   - (D) scour

2. The actor gets so nervous on stage that he _____ over his lines.
   - (F) sways
   - (G) stammers
   - (H) detects
   - (I) deflates

3. The breathtaking, scenic view of the mountaintop _____ Mariana.
   - (A) damaged
   - (B) analyzed
   - (C) detected
   - (D) enraptured

4. If a car tire runs over a sharp object, it may become _____.
   - (F) sleek
   - (G) deflated
   - (H) fickle
   - (I) cumbersome

5. When the other team scored the winning goal, Joy looked _____ at her teammates.
   - (A) extravagantly
   - (B) boisterously
   - (C) somberly
   - (D) enraptured

© Harcourt • Grade 5

6. Tony offered to help his neighbor carry the _____ boxes into the house.

   (F) sleek

   (G) deflated

   (H) enterprising

   (I) cumbersome

7. For their class trip, the _____ students found a clever way to raise funds.

   (A) enterprising

   (B) deflated

   (C) cumbersome

   (D) vital

Name _____

Grammar: Present Tense; Subject-Verb Agreement

▶ **Choose the best answer for each question.**

1. Read this sentence.

    Taylor and Megan _____ a new library book every week.

    Which is the correct present-tense verb to use in the sentence?
    (A) selects
    (B) selecting
    (C) select
    (D) selected

2. Read this sentence.

    The family members _____ at the table to eat dinner each night.

    Which is the correct present-tense verb to use in the sentence?
    (F) convened
    (G) convene
    (H) convened
    (I) convens

3. Read this sentence.

    Patrick _____ the large envelope he is sending in the mail.

    Which is the correct present-tense verb to use in the sentence?
    (A) sealing
    (B) seals
    (C) sealed
    (D) seal

4. Read this sentence.

    A large crowd is beginning to gather around the theater.

    Which word in the sentence is a form of the verb *be*?
    (F) around
    (G) beginning
    (H) gather
    (I) is

Oral Reading Fluency

If you were to travel from the southwestern coast of Oregon down through the central coast of California, you could see something that does not grow anywhere else in the world—the remarkable redwood tree. Redwoods are some of the oldest and tallest trees on Earth. Some redwoods are more

than 1,500 years old.

A redwood tree can reach a height of over 300 feet. The trunk of a redwood is anywhere from ten to twenty feet across. Scientists do not yet understand what causes these trees to grow so large.

Redwoods are stronger than most other types of trees. Their wood contains something that prevents most insects from harming the tree. Redwoods also have a greater ability to survive fires. Adult redwoods have thick layers of bark on their trunks, which only the hottest fires can burn through. Their branches and leaves are protected because they are several hundred feet above the ground.

Although redwoods can withstand insects and fire, they are still threatened by people. Many redwoods have been cut down for lumber or to clear land for new development. Luckily, the redwoods that are located in national or state parks are protected. People can visit these parks to see one of nature's wonders.

© Harcourt • Grade 5

Selection Comprehension

▶ **Choose the best answer for each question.**

1. Which sentence BEST tells what the story is about?
   Ⓐ Mami worries about the family's missing cat.
   Ⓑ A family cat is missing for more than two weeks.
   Ⓒ Luis's band scares the family cat out of the garage.
   Ⓓ A family finds its missing cat and makes a new friend.

2. Why does Abuelita avoid answering the telephone?
   Ⓕ She prefers to speak to people in person.
   Ⓖ She thinks her only job is cooking.
   Ⓗ The calls are usually for Mami.
   Ⓘ Luis always takes the calls.

3. Who is telling the story?
   Ⓐ Abuelita
   Ⓑ Mami
   Ⓒ Arturo
   Ⓓ Rosa

4. Why does the author say there are "explosions of joy" when Leo Love calls?
   Ⓕ to show that the family is very noisy
   Ⓖ to show how everyone feels about his news
   Ⓗ to show what the family thinks about phone calls
   Ⓘ to show that Rosa and Luis have broken something

5. What does the phrase "popcorning up and down" help you understand about Rosa?
   Ⓐ She is grabbing Huitla.
   Ⓑ She likes to eat snacks.
   Ⓒ She is very excited.
   Ⓓ She likes to jump.

6. The author compares Rosa to a shooting meteor to show that she

(F) acts fast without thinking ahead.

(G) usually makes a lot of noise.

(H) often changes her mind.

(I) likes to study comets.

7. Which word BEST describes Abuelita?

(A) confused

(B) solemn

(C) dainty

(D) caring

8. How do you know that "Any Small Goodness" is realistic fiction?

(F) The characters have feelings that real people have.

(G) The setting takes place at a time in the past.

(H) The events are unlikely to happen in real life.

(I) The plot has details about events in a real person's life.

Written Response

9. **COMPARING TEXTS** In what ways do the Ant, the Mouse, and Leo Love act ALIKE? Use details from "Any Small Goodness," "The Ant and the Dove" and "The Lion and the Mouse" to explain your answer.

_____

_____

_____

_____

_____

Name _____

Focus Skill: Literary Devices

▶ Read the poem. Then choose the best answer for each
question.

My Tiger

I have a tiger beneath my bed,
who likes to sleep beside my head.
My pillow smells of catnip plants,
through which my tiger likes to prance.
She wakes me with a loud yow-yow,
That seems to say, "Please get up now!"
Then places both her furry paws,
upon my forehead, nose, and jaw.
Her light brown fur is striped with black,
and without warning she will attack!
To others she may seem quite fierce,
with teeth that bite and claws that pierce.
But I can tame this fearsome cat,
with just a friendly scratch or pat.
That is why this poem was written,
for Tiger, my favorite little kitten.

1. Which line from the poem appeals to the sense of sight?
   Ⓐ "That seems to say, 'Please get up now!'"
   Ⓑ "Then places both her furry paws,"
   Ⓒ "Her light brown fur is striped with black,"
   Ⓓ "But I can tame this fearsome cat,"

© Harcourt • Grade 5

2. Read these lines from the poem.

> To others she may seem quite fierce,
> with teeth that bite and claws that pierce.

Which sense do these lines appeal to?

(F) sight

(G) hearing

(H) touch

(I) smell

3. Which line from the poem appeals to the sense of hearing?

(A) "who likes to sleep beside my head."

(B) "She wakes me with a loud yow-yow,"

(C) "upon my forehead, nose, and jaw."

(D) "with just a friendly scratch or pat."

4. Read these lines from the poem.

> My pillow smells of catnip plants,
> through which my tiger likes to prance.

Which sense do these lines appeal to?

(F) sight

(G) hearing

(H) touch

(I) smell

Focus Skill: Literary Devices

TOTAL SCORE: _____ /4

© Harcourt • Grade 5

Literary Patterns and Symbols

▶ **Read the passage. Then choose the best answer for each question.**

Squirrel Learns a Lesson

One afternoon Squirrel was playing in the forest when he found a path that he had never explored. He discovered heaps of acorns lying among the roots of an oak tree, so he bounded down the path and gathered the nuts.

Squirrel brought the acorns home, but he was dissatisfied when he realized that his pile was not very large. Outside, the sun was setting, but Squirrel's greed got the better of him, and he decided to return to the path for more acorns. On his way, Squirrel saw Badger and told him of his plans.

Badger said, "Squirrel, autumn has arrived, and the sun sets much earlier. Many animals have lost their way in the woods!" However, Squirrel believed that he was the swiftest animal in the woods and that he could return home long before dark. He told Badger not to worry.

When Squirrel reached the oak tree, he discovered that no acorns remained, so he wandered farther down the path. Soon it became dark, and Squirrel lost his way; then he recalled Badger's warning. Just then, Squirrel was terrified by an unfamiliar sound.

"Squirrel, do not be afraid," said Cricket, who was approaching Squirrel. "I can find my way in the dark, and I will help you return to your burrow." After that, Squirrel knew that he would never ignore the advice of his friends again.

1. What qualities does Squirrel represent?
   - (A) laziness and pride
   - (B) intelligence and curiosity
   - (C) carelessness and greed
   - (D) strength and courage

© Harcourt • Grade 5

2. What quality does Cricket represent?

(F) cleverness

(G) patience

(H) kindness

(I) strength

3. Where in the story does the lesson become clear?

(A) in the first paragraph

(B) in the second paragraph

(C) in the fourth paragraph

(D) in the last paragraph

4. What is the lesson of this story?

(F) Always show kindness toward friends.

(G) It is always best to tell the truth.

(H) Remember to plan for the future.

(I) Listen to the advice of others.

Literary Patterns and Symbols

212

TOTAL SCORE: _____ /4

© Harcourt • Grade 5

Name _____

Robust Vocabulary

▶ **Choose the best word to complete each sentence.**

1. Before we host our family gatherings, my father _____ around the house to get things done.

   (A) gouges

   (B) bustles

   (C) enraptures

   (D) monopolizes

2. By focusing on positive thoughts, Juan can _____ his nervousness.

   (F) assuage

   (G) stammer

   (H) damage

   (I) gouge

3. Every time we move the desk, it _____ the floor, leaving terrible marks in the wood.

   (A) enraptures

   (B) analyzes

   (C) bustles

   (D) gouges

4. The loyal fans greeted their favorite singer with great _____ when she walked onto the stage.

   (F) bustling

   (G) damage

   (H) fervor

   (I) basking

© Harcourt • Grade 5

5. Cassie's room was always cluttered, while Arnie's room was always _____.

 Ⓐ deflated
 Ⓑ desolate
 Ⓒ enterprising
 Ⓓ immaculate

6. When Tamara's best friend was away for the entire summer, she felt _____.

 Ⓕ desolate
 Ⓖ immaculate
 Ⓗ enterprising
 Ⓘ cumbersome

© Harcourt • Grade 5

Name _____

Grammar: Past and Future Tenses

▶ **Choose the best answer for each question.**

1. Read this sentence.

   Inez _____ her new neighbors yesterday.

   Which is the correct past-tense verb to use in the sentence?
   (A) greet
   (B) greeted
   (C) greets
   (D) greeting

2. Read this sentence.

   I _____ my research paper tomorrow.

   Which is the correct future-tense verb to use in the sentence?
   (F) will write
   (G) write
   (H) wrote
   (I) have written

3. Which is the past-tense form of the verb *navigate*?
   (A) navigating
   (B) will navigate
   (C) would navigate
   (D) navigated

4. Which is the future-tense form of the verb *transmit*?
   (F) transmitting
   (G) transmits
   (H) will transmit
   (I) has transmitted

Grammar: Past and Future Tenses   215   TOTAL SCORE: _____ /4

© Harcourt • Grade 5

Oral Reading Fluency

"Ouch!" Jasmine yelped, rubbing her elbow. She had just bumped it on the ground. All afternoon, her older sister Hannah had been teaching her to ride a skateboard.

Hannah ran to retrieve the skateboard, which was rolling swiftly down the road. Jasmine scowled angrily at the wooden board in her sister's hand.

"I give up, Hannah," Jasmine said. "You make it look so effortless, but I just don't have the ability." Jasmine appreciated her sister's instruction, but she was embarrassed by her repeated failures. Overcome by frustration, she pulled off her helmet. As she began walking back down the road toward their house, Hannah ran to stop her.

"Jasmine," she said, "I know this is hard, but there is no easy way around it. You just need to be determined and concentrate on the tips I gave you. I am sure that if you practice routinely, you will develop into an excellent skateboarder."

Jasmine listened to her sister's reasonable advice, and she was filled with gratitude. She put her helmet back on, snatched the skateboard from Hannah, and gave a tremendous push with her right foot. She sped off down the road, and behind her she heard Hannah's encouraging cheers. She felt triumphant as she rode the entire way to her driveway without falling.

© Harcourt • Grade 5

Name _____

Selection Comprehension

▶ **Choose the best answer for each question.**

1. How do you know that "Chester Cricket's Pigeon Ride" is a fantasy?
   - (A) The story events are unlikely to happen in real life.
   - (B) The plot has a lesson about life.
   - (C) The setting is familiar to most readers.
   - (D) The author expresses personal opinions.

2. What is the main idea in "Chester Cricket's Pigeon Ride"?
   - (F) A cricket enjoys visiting a large city.
   - (G) Two friends explore New York City together.
   - (H) A pigeon spends a lot of time flying around a city.
   - (I) The Empire State Building is a dangerous place for animals.

3. Why does Lulu take Chester on a tour?
   - (A) She wants to be friendly to Chester.
   - (B) She thinks Chester's life is too dull.
   - (C) She wants to show off her flying talents.
   - (D) She wants to prove she knows more than Chester.

4. Why does Central Park fill Chester's heart with joy?
   - (F) It has a pretty, shimmering lake.
   - (G) It has trees he has never seen before.
   - (H) It makes him think of his drainpipe.
   - (I) It reminds him of his Connecticut home.

5. What can you conclude about Chester?
   - (A) He has flown on a pigeon's claw before.
   - (B) He often visits the shops on Fifth Avenue.
   - (C) He is curious and has a sense of adventure.
   - (D) He has always wanted to visit Central Park.

6. Which idea BEST shows that Chester is happy in Central Park?

(F) He sees a crescent moon.

(G) He chirps to his heart's content.

(H) He listens to nighttime sounds.

(I) He recognizes different kinds of trees.

7. The author says that "skyscrapers rise up like a grove of steel trees" to show that buildings in the city are

(A) cold and smooth.

(B) strong and sturdy.

(C) close together and tall.

(D) hard and made of metal.

8. Which would MOST help a reader understand the ideas in this story?

(F) looking at photographs of pigeons

(G) going on a tour of sights in New York City

(H) reading a science book about crickets

(I) making a collection of leaves from different trees

Written Response

9. Choose one word to describe Chester, and explain why you chose it. Use details from "Chester Cricket's Pigeon Ride" to support your answer.

_____

_____

_____

_____

Name _____

Focus Skill: Literary Devices

▶ **Read the passage. Then choose the best answer for each question.**

The Ice Storm

The storm painted everything with a thick layer of snow, encrusted by a layer of ice. The world sparkled like crystal, so Rafael and Nina bundled up in their warmest clothes and went out to explore their yard along with their dog, Pita.

The ice had formed a hard crust on top of the snow, strong enough to support the children. Delighted, Rafael and Nina ran and slid across the icy snow while Pita barked and chased them. Nina remembered the small hill in the woods directly behind their house, so they set off through the frozen yard. The gentle slope was as slippery as a slide, and the two children and their dog sped down it at record-breaking speed.

When they reached the bottom, Rafael shouted, "That was amazing! Let's do it again!" He and Nina began climbing up the hill, stopping to toss ice chunks at tree trunks and rocks. Pita tried to follow them, but her claws could not dig into the ice, and she repeatedly slid back to the bottom.

Nina and Rafael quickly realized their mistake. To return home, they had to walk all the way out to the road, where the snow had been removed. It was so far that their legs were stone by the time they returned to their house. They decided that they would plan ahead before their next outdoor adventure.

1. Which phrase from the passage is an example of a simile?
   Ⓐ "The storm painted everything with a layer of snow,"
   Ⓑ "The world sparkled like crystal,"
   Ⓒ "Rafael and Nina bundled up in their warmest clothes . . ."
   Ⓓ "Nina remembered the small hill in the woods . . ."

© Harcourt • Grade 5

2. Read this sentence from the passage.

> It was so far that their legs were stone by the time they returned to their house.

Which type of figurative language is used in this sentence?

(F) personification

(G) metaphor

(H) simile

(I) metaphor and personification

3. Which phrase from the passage is an example of personification?

(A) "The storm painted everything with a thick layer of snow,"

(B) "The ice had formed a hard crust on top of the snow,"

(C) "When they reached the bottom, Rafael shouted,"

(D) "To return home, they had to walk all the way out to the road,"

4. Read this sentence from the passage.

> The gentle slope was as slippery as a slide, and the two children and their dog sped down it at record-breaking speed.

Which type of figurative language is used in this sentence?

(F) personification

(G) metaphor

(H) simile

(I) personification and simile

Focus Skill: Literary Devices

TOTAL SCORE: _____ /4

© Harcourt • Grade 5

Draw Conclusions

▶ Read the passage. Then choose the best answer for each
question.

Fatima's Super Story

As Fatima and her family were driving home one afternoon, they
discussed what super abilities they would like to have. Her brother, Hadi,
said he wished that he could fly, and her father said he wished that he had
x-ray vision. Fatima decided that she would like to have both of those
powers, plus incredible strength.

When they arrived home, Fatima decided to write a story about her
super family. She searched the entire house, but she could not find a single
sheet of blank paper. She took some paper grocery bags, ripped them into
pieces, and used the blank sides to write her story.

Fatima spent the rest of the afternoon writing about her family
members and how they used their super abilities. She filled five grocery
bags before dinner, but when she saw her brother setting the table by
himself, she dragged herself away from her story to help.

After dinner, Fatima gathered her family members together. She read
her story aloud, acting out the most exciting scenes. They gave her a loud
round of applause. Then, Fatima asked her father if he would build her a
bookshelf. He asked her why she needed it, when she already had one.

"Father, we're going to need room for all the books I am going to
write," she replied. "My super family is going to be very busy!"

1. Which detail from the story shows that Fatima is creative?
   (A) She asks her father to build a bookshelf.
   (B) She helps her brother set the dinner table.
   (C) She writes her story on grocery bags.
   (D) She reads her story aloud to her family.

© Harcourt • Grade 5

2. Which detail from the story shows that Fatima is
   determined?

   (F) She wishes that she could have three super powers.

   (G) She stops writing to have dinner with her family.

   (H) She acts out the most exciting parts of her story.

   (I) She works on her story for an entire afternoon.

3. What do you learn about Fatima when she helps set the table?

   (A) She is creative and talented.

   (B) She wants to be like her brother.

   (C) She wants to have super powers.

   (D) She is kind and thoughtful.

4. What do you learn about Fatima as she reads her story to her family?

   (F) She is nervous about reading to others.

   (G) She likes acting in front of others.

   (H) She is not afraid to ask for help.

   (I) She plans to buy more writing supplies.

Draw Conclusions

222

TOTAL SCORE: _____ /4

© Harcourt • Grade 5

Robust Vocabulary

▶ **Choose the best word to complete each sentence.**

1. When he thought he had lost his sister's new book, Micha began to feel _____.
   - (A) deduction
   - (B) fervor
   - (C) pinnacle
   - (D) panic

2. After riding the roller coaster three times, Maya and Tuari felt _____ and had to sit down.
   - (F) desolate
   - (G) precious
   - (H) immaculate
   - (I) giddy

3. Kyle's aunt often took him on _____ to her favorite fishing spot.
   - (A) compartments
   - (B) excursions
   - (C) pinnacles
   - (D) devices

4. As the heavy storm swept through the area, the lake water became more _____.
   - (F) turbulent
   - (G) precious
   - (H) gleeful
   - (I) giddy

5. It takes strength and determination to climb to the _____ of the world's highest mountain.
   - (A) pinnacle
   - (B) panic
   - (C) excursion
   - (D) fervor

© Harcourt • Grade 5

Name _____

6. When her favorite cousins arrived for a surprise visit, Daniela felt _____.

   (F) immaculate

   (G) turbulent

   (H) gleeful

   (I) precious

7. Anya's family photo album was one of her most _____ possessions.

   (A) turbulent

   (B) precious

   (C) gleeful

   (D) giddy

TOTAL SCORE: _____ /7

Grammar: Verbs: Perfect Tenses

▶ **Choose the best answer for each question.**

1. Read this sentence.

   For eleven years, she _____ in the house on Palm Street.

   Which is the correct present-perfect-tense verb to use in the sentence?
   (A) has resided
   (B) have resided
   (C) had resided
   (D) will have resided

2. Read this sentence.

   I was so proud that I _____ my homework every night this week.

   Which is the correct past-perfect-tense verb to use in the sentence?
   (F) has finished
   (G) have finished
   (H) had finished
   (I) will have finished

3. Read this sentence.

   By the end of next week, the detective _____ all her open leads.

   Which is the correct future-perfect-tense verb to use in the sentence?
   (A) has investigated
   (B) have investigated
   (C) had investigated
   (D) will have investigated

4. Read this sentence.

   It is great that you _____ every soccer practice this season.

   Which is the correct present-perfect tense verb to use in the sentence?
   (F) has attended
   (G) have attended
   (H) had attended
   (I) will have attended

Grammar: Verbs: Perfect Tenses

225

TOTAL SCORE: _____ /4

Oral Reading Fluency

If you enjoy being outdoors, you will love visiting Mount Desert Island in Maine. This island is the location of Acadia National Park, that provides many enjoyable and adventurous activities for nature lovers.

For people who enjoy hiking, this island is an ideal place to visit. Many miles of hiking trails cover the island, winding through forests, along rocky beaches, and up tall mountains. Each mountaintop offers splendid views of the island.

For a hiking challenge, take one of the many routes up Cadillac Mountain, the highest peak on the entire eastern coast of the United States. This peak can also be reached by road, allowing more people to enjoy the view from the top.

If you want to explore the island by bicycle, there are forty-five miles of carriage roads. These roads are now used as trails reserved for biking, walking, and horseback-riding. Whichever way you decide to travel in the park, just be careful to follow this important rule: take only pictures, and leave only footprints.

At the end of the day, when you are tired and hungry, you can drive to Bar Harbor, a small city with restaurants, shops, and hotels. Any trip to this amazing island is sure to leave you with many special memories.

© Harcourt • Grade 5

Name _____

Selection Comprehension

▶ **Choose the best answer for each question.**

1. Why did the author write "The Compassion Campaign"?
   - (A) to persuade people to start community gardens
   - (B) to explain how to volunteer in a neighborhood
   - (C) to show how students can help their community
   - (D) to explain how a television program is put together

2. The author would be MOST LIKELY to agree that
   - (F) life as a fifth grader is difficult.
   - (G) old-fashioned gardens are best.
   - (H) any one person can make a difference.
   - (I) television programs usually do a lot of good.

3. When T. J. Mark says, "I hear you've taken your show on the road," he means that Brent has
   - (A) put on a show in a different location.
   - (B) started performing beside a highway.
   - (C) moved his equipment to another garage.
   - (D) set up a stage on the street in front of his house.

4. The parts of the Friends and Family are MAINLY used to
   - (F) add more details to the dialogue.
   - (G) explain how the characters feel.
   - (H) describe the characters' actions.
   - (I) solve the story problem.

5. Which detail would be MOST important to include in a summary of "The Compassion Campaign"?
   - (A) Birds under stress may lose all their feathers.
   - (B) The reporters interview students across the county.
   - (C) Sheila went on a trip to Costa Rica with her uncle.
   - (D) One of the main characters is named Penny Baldwin.

6. Which word BEST describes Brent, the boy who plays guitar?

    (F) critical

    (G) distinguished

    (H) humorous

    (I) thoughtful

7. How are all the students interviewed ALIKE?

    (A) All have worked in backyard gardens.

    (B) All want to make the world a better place.

    (C) All repair houses to help homeless families.

    (D) All work to gain the trust of frightened animals.

8. Penny Baldwin's next television show will be about students who

    (F) are famous artists in a big city.

    (G) take painting classes at an art school.

    (H) paint pictures on buildings to brighten a neighborhood.

    (I) have entered a contest to draw pictures on the sidewalk.

READ THINK EXPLAIN **Written Response**

9. Imagine that you could help one of the students interviewed in "The Compassion Campaign" with his or her project. Tell which student you would choose, and explain why you would make that choice. Use details to support your answer.

_____

_____

_____

_____

Name _____

Robust Vocabulary

▶ **Choose the best word to complete each sentence.**

1. Megan is a kind, helpful girl who has never _____ other people.
   - (A) bustled
   - (B) mistreated
   - (C) mentored
   - (D) stammered

2. The townspeople raised money to repair the old, _____ town hall building.
   - (F) precious
   - (G) bland
   - (H) dilapidated
   - (I) compassionate

3. Carmen and Pablo love cooking with their father, but they _____ cleaning up the mess.
   - (A) gouge
   - (B) loathe
   - (C) mistreat
   - (D) assuage

4. Miguel likes foods that are flavorful, rather than those that are _____.
   - (F) bland
   - (G) dilapidated
   - (H) deflated
   - (I) turbulent

5. Tyrone is a good dancer because he has both rhythm and _____.
   - (A) coordination
   - (B) sensibility
   - (C) altruism
   - (D) advocacy

Robust Vocabulary

229

© Harcourt • Grade 5

6. When Matthew kindly gave his seat on the bus to a man carrying an infant, he showed _____.

   (F) coordination

   (G) altruism

   (H) advocacy

   (I) panic

7. Kendra's artwork shows that she has a _____ for colors and patterns.

   (A) pinnacle

   (B) assuage

   (C) coordination

   (D) sensibility

8. Because Partha always offers help to other people in need, he is _____.

   (F) giddy

   (G) bland

   (H) compassionate

   (I) dilapidated

9. Mrs. Read is a good _____ to Juanita because she gives Juanita support and advice.

   (A) sensibility

   (B) excursion

   (C) pinnacle

   (D) mentor

10. On Earth Day, many groups use _____ to encourage others to preserve nature.

   (F) advocacy

   (G) enterprise

   (H) pinnacles

   (I) coordination

Name _____

Selection Comprehension

▶ **Choose the best answer for each question.**

1. How do you know that "Lewis and Clark" is narrative nonfiction?
    (A) The plot teaches a lesson about life.
    (B) The characters, places, and events are real.
    (C) The plot has a beginning, a middle, and an ending.
    (D) The author's personal thoughts and feelings are included.

2. Why do you think the author wrote "Lewis and Clark"?
    (F) to explain why people become explorers
    (G) to inform readers about a route to the Pacific Ocean
    (H) to tell about something Thomas Jefferson had requested
    (I) to describe an important event in the history of the United States

3. Why were mountain ranges and waterfalls troublesome for Lewis and Clark?
    (A) They had to map the location of each mountain and waterfall.
    (B) The trails near rivers and mountains were full of wild animals.
    (C) Getting around the mountains and waterfalls would be hard and take time.
    (D) Seeing mountains and waterfalls meant they were lost.

4. What is the MOST likely reason the Shoshone at first refused to give Lewis and Clark horses?
    (F) They needed the horses to carry supplies.
    (G) They did not want the explorers to reach the coast.
    (H) They feared the men might be friendly with the Blackfeet.
    (I) They did not understand what the explorers were requesting.

5. Why did Cameahwait change his mind about giving horses to the explorers?
    (A) Lewis explained how important their expedition was.
    (B) Sacagawea recognized the chief as a member of her family.
    (C) A letter from Thomas Jefferson requested the Cameahwaits' help.
    (D) Members of the village decided they should help the travelers.

**Selection Comprehension
"Lewis and Clark"**

© Harcourt • Grade 5

6. Which detail is MOST important to include in a summary of "Lewis and Clark"?

(F) The men traveled on many beautiful rivers.

(G) Sacagawea carried her baby during the trip.

(H) Lewis and Clark met the Shoshone.

(I) Sacagawea helped by finding food and landmarks.

7. How are the ideas in "Lewis and Clark" MOSTLY organized?

(A) events in time order

(B) a problem and a solution

(C) how two things are alike

(D) causes and effects

8. Which sentence BEST summarizes the main ideas of "Lewis and Clark"?

(F) Lewis and Clark made important discoveries in the territory between St. Louis and the Pacific Ocean.

(G) The journey of Lewis and Clark to the mouth of the Columbia River took two years.

(H) President Thomas Jefferson believed that the explorers would find a river that led to the Pacific Ocean.

(I) The explorers brought back stories about huge grizzly bears and high mountain passes.

Written Response

9. Explain why you would or would not have liked to be a member of the Corps of Discovery. Use details from "Lewis and Clark" to support your answer.

_____

_____

_____

_____

Focus Skill: Summarize and Paraphrase

▶ **Read the passage. Then choose the best answer for each
question.**

Sea Cucumbers

You might think that a sea cucumber is a salad vegetable similar to a
carrot, but it is actually a living creature. It belongs to the same family of
animals as the starfish. It earned its name due to its body, which is long
and narrow, like a cucumber.

All sea cucumbers are not alike. For example, they come in different
sizes, from shorter than one inch to about six feet long. They also live in
different parts of the ocean. Some live in the shallow water along beaches,
while others live in the deepest areas of the ocean floor. Finally, they move
differently. A few sea cucumbers can swim, while others seem to simply
float along with the ocean currents.

Sea cucumbers have two unusual ways of protecting themselves. When
they feel threatened, they can spit out their organs, which confuses and
frightens other animals without harming the sea cucumber. Once the sea
cucumber has escaped, its organs quickly grow back. Some sea cucumbers
can also scare off enemies by releasing thin threads that are as sticky as glue.

Sea cucumbers are important in the chain of life in the world's oceans.
They feed partly on the waste of other creatures, helping to keep oceans
clean. Many other fish depend on their eggs for food. Sea cucumbers even
provide a home for some very small types of worms, fish, and crabs.

1. Read this sentence from the article.

   **It earned its name due to its body, which is long and
   narrow, like a cucumber.**

   Which of the following best paraphrases the sentence above?

   Ⓐ It is named after the cucumber because its body is shaped like a
   cucumber.

   Ⓑ It earned its name due to its body, which is long and narrow, like
   a cucumber.

   Ⓒ Its body is long like a cucumber, for which it is named because it is
   long, too.

   Ⓓ It is named after a cucumber rather than being a cucumber.

Focus Skill: Summarize and Paraphrase   233

2. Which of the following best summarizes paragraph 2?

(F) Sea cucumbers live in both the deepest and most shallow parts of the ocean.

(G) Sea cucumbers differ in how large they grow, where they live, and how they move.

(H) Sea cucumbers can grow large or small, and they can move in different ways.

(I) Sea cucumbers move by swimming or floating, and they can grow to different sizes.

3. Read this sentence from the article.

> **Some sea cucumbers can also scare off enemies by releasing thin threads that are as sticky as glue.**

Which of the following best paraphrases the sentence above?

(A) Some sea cucumbers use different ways of protecting themselves from other sea creatures.

(B) Some sea cucumbers can also scare off enemies by releasing thin threads that are as sticky as glue.

(C) Some sea cucumbers can give off glue-like strings that frighten away other sea creatures.

(D) All sea cucumbers can scare off other sea cucumbers by releasing sticky threads that are like glue.

4. Which of the following best summarizes paragraph 4?

(F) Other animals, such as some types of fish, crabs, and worms, feed on sea cucumbers.

(G) Other sea animals depend on sea cucumbers for food, clean water, and a place to live.

(H) Sea cucumbers feed on the waste of other animals, which cleans the ocean water.

(I) Sea cucumbers keep the ocean clean and provide food and shelter for other animals.

Focus Skill: Summarize and Paraphrase   234   **TOTAL SCORE:** _____ /4

© Harcourt • Grade 5

Robust Vocabulary

▶ **Choose the best word to complete each sentence.**

1. Because she is an excellent musician, Lucia is a great _____ to the school band.
   (A) peril
   (B) terrain
   (C) asset
   (D) ordeal

2. Mr. Shaw was so proud of his students that he praised them _____ for all of their hard work.
   (F) somberly
   (G) intently
   (H) blandly
   (I) profusely

3. It is best to wear sturdy shoes when walking on steep or rocky _____.
   (A) terrain
   (B) ordeal
   (C) asset
   (D) peril

4. Liz looked both ways before crossing the busy street to avoid putting herself in _____.
   (F) ordeal
   (G) peril
   (H) asset
   (I) terrain

5. Tobias was studying the puzzle pieces so _____ that he did not hear the phone ring.
   (A) gleefully
   (B) compassionately
   (C) profusely
   (D) intently

Robust Vocabulary

235

© Harcourt • Grade 5

6. When the movers had to carry the heavy furniture up the narrow staircase, it was a terrible _____.

   (F) ordeal

   (G) asset

   (H) terrain

   (I) mentor

7. The children decided to play inside rather than go out in the _____ weather.

   (A) precious

   (B) dilapidated

   (C) intent

   (D) dismal

8. Francisco's strength and courage caused many people to _____ him highly.

   (F) esteem

   (G) mistreat

   (H) loathe

   (I) peril

© Harcourt • Grade 5

Name _____

Grammar: Irregular Verbs

▶ **Choose the best answer for each question.**

1. Which is the past-tense form of the verb *catch*?
   - (A) caught
   - (B) catching
   - (C) catched
   - (D) catches

2. Which is the correct verb to use in this sentence?

   The new director is _____ his first show.

   - (F) broadcasted
   - (G) broadcast
   - (H) boadcasten
   - (I) broadcasting

3. Which is the past-participle form of the verb *swim*?
   - (A) have swimming
   - (B) have swum
   - (C) have swam
   - (D) have swimmed

4. Which is the correct verb to use in this sentence?

   Yesterday the player _____ from the competition.

   - (F) withdraws
   - (G) withdrawing
   - (H) withdrawn
   - (I) withdrew

Grammar: Irregular Verbs

237

TOTAL SCORE: _____ /4

Oral Reading Fluency

Sun tapped the tip of her pencil on the blank sheet of paper before her and closed her eyes, hoping a story would suddenly spring into her mind. She had heard that people sometimes ran out of ideas for a period of time in what was called "writer's block," and now it was happening to her.

First, she asked her sister Min for advice. Min suggested that Sun draw the first picture that came into her mind and write a story based on the picture. Sun drew a picture of herself sitting at a desk with a large question mark floating over her head, but that did not help her write a story.

Next, Sun asked her brother Jin what he did when he had writer's block. He told her that he listened to one of his favorite songs and wrote about the song. Sun listened to an entire album of her favorite songs, but it made her feel like dancing instead of writing.

Finally, Sun asked her grandmother how to overcome writer's block. Her grandmother told her that the only way to solve her problem was to write about the first thing that came to mind.

Sun sat down at her desk, picked up her pencil, and wrote, "Today I experienced writer's block for the first time."

© Harcourt • Grade 5

Name _____

Selection Comprehension

▶ **Choose the best answer for each question.**

1. Why were women discouraged from going to the Klondike?
   - (A) The law did not allow them to mine for gold.
   - (B) Boats going north did not have room for them.
   - (C) The area had very few hotels and inns for them.
   - (D) The hardships might be too harsh for them to survive.

2. What BEST prepared Kate for her trip to the Klondike?
   - (F) She grew up doing a lot of hard work.
   - (G) She once worked in her father's store.
   - (H) She had helped take care of animals.
   - (I) She bought special lace-up boots.

3. How do you know "Klondike Kate" is a biography?
   - (A) The author tells her personal thoughts and feelings.
   - (B) It has information about a person's life.
   - (C) It has a setting that is familiar to most readers.
   - (D) The events could not happen in real life.

4. What was the FIRST challenge Kate faced?
   - (F) having heavy rain soak her tent and clothes
   - (G) earning enough money to build her own cabin
   - (H) finding a way to carry all her heavy food supplies
   - (I) crossing a mountain pass in extremely cold weather

5. Based on the passage, which word BEST describes Klondike Kate?
   - (A) delicate
   - (B) obedient
   - (C) humorous
   - (D) independent

6. Why do you think the author wrote "Klondike Kate"?

(F) to inform readers about the Gold Rush

(G) to tell readers about a very brave woman

(H) to describe the problems of gold miners

(I) to explain what life was like in the nineteenth ceentury

7. Which fact would be MOST important to include in a summary of "Klondike Kate"?

(A) Kate took the dangerous overland route to the Yukon.

(B) Kate knew many people on the Alaskan frontier.

(C) Kate was the youngest of seven children.

(D) Kate did not like living in a city.

8. What did Kate do with the five-dollar gold piece her friends asked her to invest?

(F) bought supplies for her trip

(G) purchased huskies and a sled

(H) started a restaurant in a hotel

(I) paid for a sourdough "starter"

READ THINK EXPLAIN **Written Response**

9. Explain why Kate Ryan was successful in the wild North when other people failed there. Use details from "Klondike Kate" to support your answer.

_____

_____

_____

_____

_____

Name _____

Focus Skill: Summarize and Paraphrase

▶ **Read the passage. Then choose the best answer for each question.**

North American river otters are thought of as playful animals. A mother and her young can sometimes be seen enjoying themselves sliding down snow-covered or muddy hills. They also play in the water. Many of these playful activities serve a purpose. Sliding is a quick way for adult otters to travel. Mother otters teach their babies important skills, such as hunting, through play.

Otters are most comfortable in water but can travel on land. They are excellent swimmers that move through the water by propelling themselves with their powerful tails. Otters also have webbed feet that help them swim and eat. They also have ears and noses that they close to keep water out when they are underwater. Otters can also run quickly on land, which helps them escape predators.

Otters like to live near lakes, slow-moving rivers, or streams where they can easily find food. They build dens near the water's edge. This allows them to make an underwater entrance to their home. Otters' homes also have a tunnel that leads to a nesting area.

Otters usually hunt at night but can also be seen hunting during the day. They like to eat fish. They will also eat crabs, turtles, and crayfish. They even eat frogs, snakes and birds or their eggs when necessary.

Otters can swim quickly and usually prey on slower-moving fish. Otters use their long whiskers to help them feel movement in the water to find fish in dark water. Otters usually eat their prey in the water. They will eat larger prey on shore.

1. How can you summarize the first paragraph?
   (A) River otters are playful animals.
   (B) Adult otters slide down hills to travel more quickly.
   (C) Mother otters teach their babies to swim and hunt.
   (D) Otters engage in playful activities that serve a purpose.

© Harcourt • Grade 5

2. Read this sentence from the article.

> Otters can also run quickly on land, which helps them
> escape predators.

How can you paraphrase this line?

(F) Otters can also run quickly on land, which helps them escape predators.

(G) Otters escape predators by running and swimming quickly.

(H) Otters are as quick on land as in the water, which helps them.

(I) Otters keep safe from predators on land because they are able to move quickly.

3. How can you summarize the third paragraph?

(A) Otters build homes near water where they can find food and have easy access to and from their homes.

(B) Otters choose to live near lakes, rivers, and streams so they can find fish.

(C) Otters build their dens near water, because they are excellent swimmers.

(D) Otters use tunnels to get from their homes to the water to find food.

4. Read this sentence from the article.

> Otters can swim quickly and usually prey
> on slower-moving fish.

How can you paraphrase this line?

(F) Otters are natural swimmers that eat fish.

(G) Even though otters can swim quickly, they usually prey on slower-moving fish.

(H) Slow-moving fish make up most of an otter's diet.

(I) Otters hunt fish that swim slowly, despite the fact that otters swim well.

Focus Skill: Summarize and Paraphrase   242   TOTAL SCORE: _____ /4

Robust Vocabulary

▶ **Choose the best word to complete each sentence.**

1. As he walked up his driveway through the thick mud,
   Antonio _____.
   (A) assuaged
   (B) floundered
   (C) esteemed
   (D) appalled

2. Riding in a car for ten hours without stopping would be a _____
   experience.
   (F) grueling
   (G) loathe
   (H) compassionate
   (I) mistreat

3. As she looked at the amount of trash scattered around the park, Aisha
   was _____.
   (A) appalled
   (B) floundered
   (C) dilapidated
   (D) isolated

4. The moving truck was _____ with all of the family's belongings.
   (F) bland
   (G) remote
   (H) laden
   (I) dismal

© Harcourt • Grade 5

5. National parks allow people to explore _____ areas that are far from large cities.

- (A) remote
- (B) grueling
- (C) dismal
- (D) dilapidated

6. The teacher encouraged her students to _____ one hour each day in reading for fun.

- (F) mistreat
- (G) loathe
- (H) flounder
- (I) invest

7. Because of the extreme heat, deserts are often _____ places with few cities or towns.

- (A) isolated
- (B) appalled
- (C) precious
- (D) turbulent

© Harcourt • Grade 5

Name _____

Grammar: Contractions

▶ **Choose the best answer for each question.**

1. Which contraction can replace *we are* in this sentence?

   Tomorrow, we are eating lunch together in the cafeteria.

   (A) we're
   (B) we've
   (C) were
   (D) wear

2. Which word can replace *they are* in this sentence?

   In the morning, they are going to the library to check out
   some books.

   (F) their
   (G) there
   (H) they've
   (I) they're

3. Which contraction can replace *did not* in this sentence?

   He did not have a turn running around the track course.

   (A) doesn't
   (B) didn't
   (C) don't
   (D) did'nt

4. Which contraction can replace *have not* in this sentence?

   We have not seen the newest movie playing in theaters.

   (F) have'nt
   (G) has'nt
   (H) haven't
   (I) hasn't

TOTAL SCORE: _____ /4

© Harcourt • Grade 5

Oral Reading Fluency

Nellie Bly was a famous American reporter and a successful businesswoman during the 1880s, 1890s, and early 1900s. In both of these occupations, she was committed to improving the lives of her fellow citizens.

Born in 1864 as Elizabeth Cochrane, her real name was changed to Nellie Bly when she took her first job as a reporter. At that time, many women writers did not use their real names.

Her first reporting job was for the *Pittsburgh Dispatch*. Later, Nellie Bly moved to New York, where she worked for a popular newspaper called *New York World*. She founded a new style of reporting, which resembled detective work because she did investigative work to find out the truth about important events.

One of Nellie Bly's most famous articles was about hospitals in New York. In her article, she described the poor treatment people received in hospitals, and because of her work, hospital care was improved. After this article was published, some people believed she was America's best reporter.

Nellie Bly also helped improve the lives of factory workers. She took over two companies that had been run by her husband, and she found that people worked better when they were happy and healthy. She had gyms and libraries put in at both companies. Due to these changes, many people began to enjoy their jobs.

© Harcourt • Grade 5

Selection Comprehension

▶ **Choose the best answer for each question.**

1. Which sentence from the selection expresses an OPINION?

   (A) Its summit is the highest point on earth, 5-1/2 miles above sea level.

   (B) Mount Everest is a place of great beauty, adventure, and danger.

   (C) Nepal, a small country that borders India, is the home of the Sherpa people.

   (D) The earth's continents are always moving, drifting slowly together or apart.

2. How do you know that "The Top of the World" is nonfiction?

   (F) It is set in the future and has technology of the future.

   (G) It has headings that begin sections of related information.

   (H) It gives details about important events in the author's life.

   (I) It reveals characters' actions and feelings through dialogue.

3. With which statement would the author MOST LIKELY agree?

   (A) Without Sherpas, people would be unable to climb mountains.

   (B) The gear needed to climb mountains is heavy and expensive.

   (C) People who climb Mount Everest face hardships and challenges.

   (D) Flying over Mount Everest is often both frightening and dangerous.

4. Which sentence BEST states the main idea of "The Top of the World"?

   (F) Mount Everest is the highest mountain on the earth.

   (G) A great deal of equipment is needed to climb Mount Everest.

   (H) Cold temperatures on Mount Everest create problems for climbers.

   (I) Adventurers must prepare very carefully when climbing Mount Everest.

5. Why would most climbers wear glacier glasses?

   (A) to see where they are walking

   (B) to keep warm

   (C) to help protect their eyes

   (D) to see clearly in high altitudes

6. Why are the Sherpas successful guides?

(F) They know how to raise and train yaks.

(G) They knew the first British adventurers.

(H) They are used to being in high altitudes.

(I) They are experienced at packing gear.

7. Why would most climbers need an oxygen tank and mask?

(A) to help stay warm

(B) to avoid getting dizzy

(C) to keep balance on the ice

(D) to stop sliding down a mountain

8. The author says the trip from Kathmandu to base camp is like "traveling from the tropics to the Arctic" MAINLY to

(F) point out the extreme temperature changes.

(G) show which animals live at high altitudes.

(H) explain why trees stop growing at one point.

(I) describe how breathing becomes difficult.

Written Response

9. **COMPARING TEXTS** Use information from BOTH "The Top of the World" and "On Top of the World" to describe some problems Edmund Hillary and Tenzing Norgay faced when climbing Mount Everest.

_____

_____

_____

_____

_____

Name _____

Focus Skill: Fact and Opinion

▶ Read the passage. Then choose the best answer for each question.

You Can't Beat Spring in New England

Spring is by far the best season in New England. The sun's heat becomes stronger, the snow melts, and flowers start to bloom. The days get longer and warmer as summer approaches, and the landscape is filled with green leaves and colorful flowers.

The temperature in parts of New England can rise very high in the summer months. In fact, the hottest summer temperature in the city of Boston, Massachusetts, was 104 degrees, which occurred on July 4, 1911. Unless you can spend your days cooling off, summers in parts of this area are simply too hot.

Similar to spring, autumn is a time of great change in New England. Though the days can still be warm, the temperature drops at night. The leaves change from green to red, orange, yellow, or brown before they drop. Autumn is a beautiful season, but it leads to winter too quickly.

Winters are usually cold in New England, and the temperature often goes below freezing. Each day has fewer hours of daylight until the shortest day of the year, in December. Overall, winters in New England are too cold and too dark.

As you can see, no other season is as enjoyable as spring in New England. Spring is the best, because it means that winter is over and summer is on the way.

1. Which sentence from the passage is a fact?
   Ⓐ "Unless you can spend your days cooling off, summers in parts of this area are simply too hot."
   Ⓑ "Though the days can still be warm, the temperature drops at night."
   Ⓒ "Autumn is a beautiful season, but it leads to winter too quickly."
   Ⓓ "As you can see, no other season is as enjoyable as spring in New England."

© Harcourt • Grade 5

2. Which sentence from the passage is an opinion?

(F) "The sun's heat becomes stronger, the snow melts, and flowers start to bloom."

(G) "Similar to spring, autumn is a time of great change in New England."

(H) "The leaves change from green to red, orange, yellow, or brown before they drop."

(I) "Spring is the best, because it means that winter is over and summer is on the way."

3. Read this statement from the passage.

Overall, winters in New England are too cold and too dark.

Why is this statement an opinion?

(A) It gives information that can be proven on the Internet.

(B) It tries to persuade you to dislike wintertime in New England.

(C) It show how the author feels about New England winters.

(D) It gives details about New England winter weather.

4. Read this statement from the passage.

In fact, the hottest summer temperature in the city of Boston, Massachusetts, was 104 degrees, which occurred on July 4, 1911.

Why is this statement a fact?

(F) It tells where the information about the weather in Boston was found.

(G) It describes how the author feels about summers in New England.

(H) It shows why the author thinks that summers are too hot in New England.

(I) It can be proven to be true by looking up facts about Boston weather.

Focus Skill: Fact and Opinion

250

TOTAL SCORE: _____ /4

© Harcourt • Grade 5

Name _____

Graphic Sources

▶ Study both graphs. Then choose the best answer for
each question.

Mr. Chen's Fifth Grade Class:
Students' Favorite Subjects

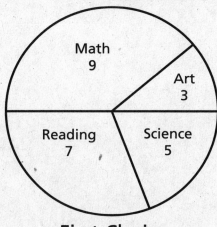

First Choice

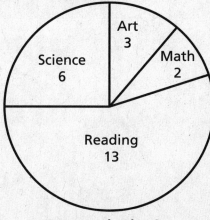

Second Choice

1. How many students are in Mr. Chen's fifth grade class?
   - (A) 9
   - (B) 13
   - (C) 24
   - (D) 48

2. How many students made reading their first choice?
   - (F) 7
   - (G) 13
   - (H) 9
   - (I) 5

3. How many students made reading their second choice?
   - (A) 7
   - (B) 3
   - (C) 6
   - (D) 13

Graphic Sources

© Harcourt • Grade 5

4. Which subject did most students make their first choice?

(F) art

(G) math

(H) science

(I) reading

TOTAL SCORE: _____ /4

Name _____

Robust Vocabulary

▶ **Choose the best word to complete each sentence.**

1. To help the craft move easily through water, a sailboat's
   shape is _____.
   - (A) accustomed
   - (B) streamlined
   - (C) grueling
   - (D) remote

2. Using sunscreen or a hat is _____ to protect your skin from sunburn.
   - (F) remote
   - (G) precious
   - (H) secure
   - (I) essential

3. Before she ran down the field, Kelly made sure she had a _____ grip
   on the football.
   - (A) secure
   - (B) streamlined
   - (C) dismal
   - (D) bland

4. After several swimming lessons, Carmen was _____ to being in
   the water.
   - (F) panicked
   - (G) appalled
   - (H) streamlined
   - (I) accustomed

Robust Vocabulary

© Harcourt • Grade 5

Name _____

5. Manuel could see far over the surrounding towns from
the _____ of the mountain.
- (A) peril
- (B) streamline
- (C) summit
- (D) terrain

6. A polar bear could not live in the desert because it could not _____ itself
to the hot weather.
- (F) acclimate
- (G) invest
- (H) flounder
- (I) secure

© Harcourt • Grade 5

Name _____

Grammar: Adverbs

▶ **Choose the best answer for each question.**

1. Which is the correct adverb phrase to use in this sentence?

    You should speak _____ in a library than on the playground.

    (A) more quiet
    (B) more quietest
    (C) more quieter
    (D) more quietly

2. Which is the correct adverb to use in this sentence?

    He arrived _____ than expected at the business meeting.

    (F) lately
    (G) late
    (H) later
    (I) latest

3. Which is the correct verb and adverb to use in this sentence?

    Because she didn't eat breakfast, she ate the apple _____.

    (A) hunger
    (B) hungrily
    (C) hungry
    (D) hungered

4. Which is the correct adverb to use in this sentence?

    George _____ remember to bring his backpack to school.

    (F) can never
    (G) can't never
    (H) don't ever
    (I) don't never

Grammar: Adverbs

TOTAL SCORE: _____ /4

© Harcourt • Grade 5

Oral Reading Fluency

One rainy Saturday, Tavon took his little sister, Shandra, to the children's museum. She had seen pictures of Tavon posing with some of the museum exhibits when he was a young boy, and she had waited anxiously for her chance to visit.

Shandra liked the museum from the moment she spied it from the parking lot. Outside the front entrance stood an enormous statue of a milk bottle that was nearly as tall as the building, and nearby was an outdoor playground.

First, Tavon led Shandra to his favorite exhibit of the museum, the bubble room. It had several tubs of soapy water and instruments used for creating bubbles of all shapes and sizes. Shandra used a large hoop to make a bubble that was almost the same size as Tavon.

Next, Shandra chose to visit the costume closet, which was located inside of a room that resembled an attic. She sorted through closets and chests filled with clothes from different historical periods. She and Tavon laughed as they tried on various outfits.

Tavon and Shandra visited all of the exhibits, and by the end of the day they felt tired, but happy. Before they left, Tavon took a picture of Shandra in front of the giant milk bottle. Shandra thanked Tavon for sharing such an extraordinary experience with her.

© Harcourt • Grade 5

Name _____

Selection Comprehension

▶ **Choose the best answer for each question.**

1. How do you know that "The Man Who Went to the Far Side of the Moon" is nonfiction?

   Ⓐ It gives facts and details about a real event.

   Ⓑ It has a setting that is familiar to readers.

   Ⓒ It provides a lesson or a moral about life.

   Ⓓ It tells about an event that could not really happen.

2. Which sentence is a FACT?

   Ⓕ The rocket *Saturn 5* is standing on Launch Pad 39A.

   Ⓖ Everything is back to normal again.

   Ⓗ Neil thinks it smells like wet ashes.

   Ⓘ It was beautiful, but compared to Earth it was nothing.

3. Which sentence BEST states the main idea of "The Man Who Went to the Far Side of the Moon"?

   Ⓐ People all over the world watched the first man on the moon.

   Ⓑ The trip to the moon deeply affected one of the astronauts.

   Ⓒ The moon landing took a long time to accomplish.

   Ⓓ Life on the spacecraft *Columbia* was difficult.

4. Why did the author include the diagram, Apollo 11 Round-Trip to the Moon?

   Ⓕ to explain how the spacecraft and lunar module work

   Ⓖ to explain why people are so interested in space flights

   Ⓗ to show why the rocket enters a state of weightlessness

   Ⓘ to show the possible dangers involved in space travel

5. Why does the author recall the day of July 16?

   Ⓐ to explain what the trip to the moon was like

   Ⓑ to tell how long it took the rocket to take off

   Ⓒ to describe the feelings of the people watching

   Ⓓ to create a strong sense of mystery for the reader

**Selection Comprehension
"The Man Who Went to the
Far Side of the Moon"**

257

© Harcourt • Grade 5

6. What detail BEST shows that Michael Collins felt lonely in space?

   (F) He could no longer see the surface of the moon.

   (G) He slowly repeated the names of his children.

   (H) He thought that he had seen a new color.

   (I) He heard the walls squeaking a little.

7. Which sentence expresses an OPINION?

   (A) Every 120th minute he sees the Earth rise at the horizon.

   (B) He has flown airplanes by himself for almost 20 years.

   (C) It's quiet in the capsule on the dark side of the moon.

   (D) It smells like wet dogs and rotten swamp.

8. What is the MOST LIKELY reason Michael Collins gave up traveling?

   (F) He decided that raising roses was more interesting.

   (G) He thought fishing was as exciting as space missions.

   (H) He realized that Earth is a beautiful and special place.

   (I) He was upset that he did not get to set foot on the moon.

READ
THINK
EXPLAIN

Written Response

9. Explain why Michael Collins's job was difficult. Use details from "The Man Who Went to the Far Side of the Moon" to support your answer.

   _____

   _____

   _____

   _____

   _____

Selection Comprehension
"The Man Who Went to the
Far Side of the Moon"

258

TOTAL SCORE: _____ /8 + _____ /2

© Harcourt • Grade 5

Focus Skill: Fact and Opinion

▶ **Read the passage. Then choose the best answer for each question.**

The Joshua Tree

The Joshua tree is one of the most interesting and unusual trees in the world. This tall, spiky tree resembles an imaginary plant from the future. It only grows in the United States, in desert areas of the Southwest. Most of these trees are found in Joshua Tree National Park, in California.

The Joshua tree was named by settlers who came to the Southwest in the 1800s. According to legend, settlers thought that the Joshua tree looked like a man standing with his arms raised in welcome.

The Joshua tree has adapted to life in the desert in some amazing ways. For example, the tree's leaves and trunk protect it from the desert climate and allow it to save what little water it receives each year. Its roots help it survive fires, because a new tree can grow from the roots of one that has burned.

Joshua trees have been useful to the people of the Southwest. Native Americans used the thick, strong leaves to weave baskets and sandals. They also ate its flower buds and seeds. Settlers who came later used Joshua tree branches to build fences for their animals.

If you get the chance, you should visit Joshua Tree National Park to see these amazing trees. Remember to treat them with care. We must make sure these incredible trees survive for many years to come.

1. Which sentence from the passage is a fact?

   (A) "The Joshua tree is one of the most interesting and unusual trees in the world."

   (B) "It only grows in the United States, in desert areas of the Southwest."

   (C) "The Joshua tree has adapted to life in the desert in some amazing ways."

   (D) "If you get the chance, you should visit Joshua Tree National Park to see these amazing trees."

Focus Skill: Fact and Opinion

2. Which sentence from the passage is an opinion?

(F) "Most of these trees are found in Joshua Tree National Park, in California."

(G) "Native Americans used the thick, strong leaves to weave baskets and sandals."

(H) "Settlers who came later used Joshua tree branches to build fences for their animals."

(I) "We must make sure these incredible trees survive for many years to come."

3. What opinion does the author express in the passage about Joshua trees and the desert?

(A) Joshua trees should be the symbol of the Southwest.

(B) Joshua trees will make you want to live in the desert.

(C) Joshua trees are the most beautiful trees of the Southwest.

(D) Joshua trees have remarkable ways of surviving in the desert.

4. Read this statement from the passage.

> **Its roots help it survive fires, because a new tree can grow from the roots of one that has burned.**

Why is this statement a fact?

(F) It tells about the appearance of the Joshua tree.

(G) It describes one of the author's own ideas.

(H) It makes a comparison between two things.

(I) It gives information that can be proven.

Name _____

Graphic Sources

▶ Study the time line. Then choose the best answer for each question.

The First 8 Weeks of a Kitten's Life

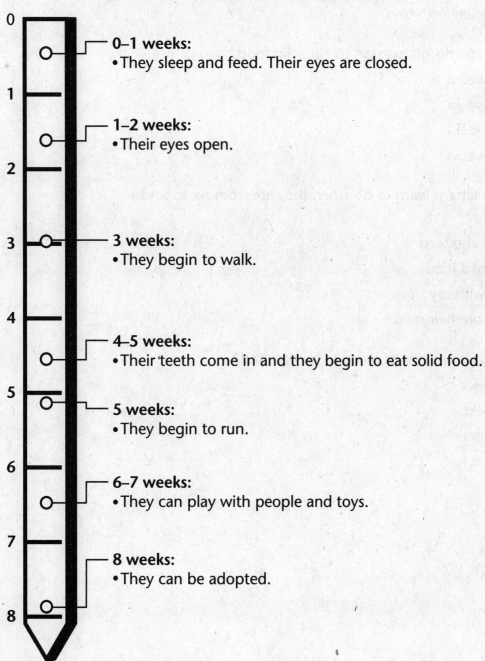

0

0–1 weeks:
• They sleep and feed. Their eyes are closed.

1

1–2 weeks:
• Their eyes open.

2

3

3 weeks:
• They begin to walk.

4

4–5 weeks:
• Their teeth come in and they begin to eat solid food.

5

5 weeks:
• They begin to run.

6

6–7 weeks:
• They can play with people and toys.

7

8 weeks:
• They can be adopted.

8

Graphic Sources

261

© Harcourt • Grade 5

1. What happens to kittens by the time they are two weeks old?

   (A) Their eyes open.

   (B) They begin to walk.

   (C) Their teeth grow in.

   (D) They play with toys.

2. At what age do kittens start to eat solid food?

   (F) 0–1 weeks

   (G) 1–2 weeks

   (H) 4–5 weeks

   (I) 6–7 weeks

3. What do kittens learn to do when they are from six to seven weeks old?

   (A) sleep and feed

   (B) eat solid food

   (C) play with toys

   (D) walk on their own

4. At what age are kittens ready to be adopted?

   (F) 2 weeks

   (G) 4 weeks

   (H) 6 weeks

   (I) 8 weeks

Graphic Sources

TOTAL SCORE: _____ /4

© Harcourt • Grade 5

Name _____

Robust Vocabulary

▶ **Choose the best word to complete each sentence.**

1. Using a long match for safety, Josefina's mother _____, the logs in the fireplace.
   - (A) ignited
   - (B) jettisoned
   - (C) acclimated
   - (D) invested

2. So the ship could gain speed, the crew _____ the heaviest baggage.
   - (F) ignited
   - (G) floundered
   - (H) streamlined
   - (I) jettisoned

3. Because he forgot to wear sunglasses, Jake was _____ in the bright sunlight.
   - (A) floundering
   - (B) squinting
   - (C) stammering
   - (D) cramping

4. When two classes combined in one classroom, the space became _____.
   - (F) dismal
   - (G) cramped
   - (H) secure
   - (I) ignited

Robust Vocabulary

© Harcourt • Grade 5

5. Visiting a calm, quiet place such as a garden gives me a
   feeling of _____.
   - (A) potential
   - (B) peril
   - (C) tranquility
   - (D) coordination

6. Attending only a few team practices before the big game
   is _____ risky.
   - (F) potentially
   - (G) essentially
   - (H) profusely
   - (I) tranquility

Grammar: Punctuation

▶ **Choose the best answer for each question.**

1. Which is the correct salutation to use at the beginning of a letter?
    (A) Dear Mrs. Rodriguez,
    (B) Dear Mrs. Rodriguez
    (C) Dear Mrs Rodriguez,
    (D) dear Mrs. Rodriguez

2. Which is the correct way to include the date on a letter?
    (F) October 18 2010,
    (G) October, 18 2010
    (H) October 18 2010
    (I) October 18, 2010

3. Which sentence uses correct punctuation?
    (A) My favorite book is flying cats.
    (B) My favorite book is Flying Cats.
    (C) My favorite book is "Flying Cats."
    (D) My favorite book is "flying cats."

4. Which sentence uses correct punctuation?
    (F) "Juan said," I like your painting.
    (G) Juan, "said I like your painting."
    (H) Juan said, "I like your painting."
    (I) Juan said "I like your painting."

TOTAL SCORE: _____ /4

© Harcourt • Grade 5

Oral Reading Fluency

Fish are fascinating creatures to watch because they often appear to be very busy, swimming back and forth as they search for food. Are they really as busy as they seem? Do they ever take time to relax?

Because some fish are almost always in motion, many people have asked the question, "Do fish ever sleep?" To discover the answer, you would have to observe fish that live in fresh water as well as those that dwell in the ocean.

To investigate the sleeping habits of fish, you would have to study fish all around the world, observing the fish both day and night to record their actions at various times of the day. What you would most likely discover is that all types of fish experience a restful state during part of the day. Because they do not have eyelids, most fish cannot close their eyes; however, they are able to rest with their eyes open.

To rest, some fish simply stop swimming and float in the water, while others rest on logs or hide among rocks. A few types of fish even lie upon the ocean floor. Some fish rest during the day, and others rest at night, but they all find some time each day to relax.

© Harcourt • Grade 5

Name _____

Selection Comprehension

▶ **Choose the best answer for each question.**

1. Which sentence BEST tells what "Exploring the Gulf Coast" is about?

   Ⓐ A captain, four explorers, and a photographer are in a small boat.

   Ⓑ The photographer must take pictures of a cottonmouth snake.

   Ⓒ The explorers have definite opinions about what they see.

   Ⓓ The captain and the explorers teach Sammy about nature.

2. What is the MOST LIKELY reason Sammy wants Captain Carolyn's help?

   Ⓕ He knows that she is familiar with the coast.

   Ⓖ He hopes she can find a cottonmouth snake.

   Ⓗ He wants her to identify different animals.

   Ⓘ He believes she has a map of the coast.

3. Sammy thinks his assignment is "nothing special" because he

   Ⓐ has taken the same pictures before.

   Ⓑ has a full week to finish the job.

   Ⓒ has to take only a few pictures.

   Ⓓ has to find only certain animals.

4. Which sentence is an OPINION from "Exploring the Gulf Coast"?

   Ⓕ Green turtles are an endangered species, and they are very
   hard to find.

   Ⓖ The cottonmouth snake is a dangerous, poisonous snake.

   Ⓗ This is going to be my best photo yet!

   Ⓘ You found all the animals!

5. Based on information from "Exploring the Gulf Coast," green turtles
   are threatened by

   Ⓐ fishing boats.

   Ⓑ limited food.

   Ⓒ polluted water.

   Ⓓ water moccasins.

6. Mangrove forests are useful MAINLY because they

(F) protect the land from heavy winds.

(G) provide homes for green turtles.

(H) are able to live in salt water.

(I) block salt with their roots.

7. The author uses both the Narrator and the Chorus to

(A) explain what the characters think.

(B) comment on what has just happened.

(C) suggest what will happen later.

(D) provide more details about the Gulf Coast.

8. Which sentence is a FACT from "Exploring the Gulf Coast"?

(F) That's the fiercest snake I've ever seen!

(G) The cottonmouth is also called a water moccasin.

(H) I believe that the variety of wildlife is what makes Florida's Gulf Coast so special!

(I) This may be a grueling experience.

Written Response

9. Imagine that you are one of the explorers on the boat. Tell what you thought was the most interesting part of the day, and explain why you thought that was most interesting.

_____

_____

_____

_____

Robust Vocabulary

▶ **Choose the best word to complete each sentence.**

1. In some countries, it is _____ to greet people by shaking hands.
   - (A) regal
   - (B) customary
   - (C) grueling
   - (D) insufficient

2. Because she always encourages the other players, Lydian is an _____ team member.
   - (F) accustomed
   - (G) insufficient
   - (H) exceptional
   - (I) isolated

3. The number of desks was _____, so the teacher added two more.
   - (A) accustomed
   - (B) insufficient
   - (C) exceptional
   - (D) dismay

4. Because he knew it was very important, Ramon worked _____ on his project.
   - (F) potentially
   - (G) exceptionally
   - (H) earnestly
   - (I) securely

5. One dozen apples is the _____ of twelve apples.
   - (A) achievement
   - (B) equivalent
   - (C) tranquility
   - (D) asset

© Harcourt • Grade 5

6. Playing music too loudly can often _____ neighbors to complain.

    (F) poise

    (G) appall

    (H) jettison

    (I) provoke

7. Learning to speak a new language is an _____ to be proud of.

    (A) investment

    (B) ordeal

    (C) equivalent

    (D) achievement

8. Jacob named his cat "Queen Kitty" because of her _____ appearance.

    (F) regal

    (G) insufficient

    (H) customary

    (I) remote

9. As soon as I turned the corner, the cat was _____ to attack my shoelaces.

    (A) cramped

    (B) poised

    (C) streamlined

    (D) provoked

10. It takes cooperation to solve a problem, not _____.

    (F) bickering

    (G) achievement

    (H) tranquility

    (I) squinting

Robust Vocabulary

TOTAL SCORE: _____ /10

© Harcourt • Grade 5